WINGS OF
FORGIVENESS

WINGS OF FORGIVENESS

Working with the Angels to
Release, Heal and Transform

KYLE GRAY

HAY HOUSE

Carlsbad, California • New York City • London • Sydney
Johannesburg • Vancouver • Hong Kong • New Delhi

First published and distributed in the United Kingdom by:
Hay House UK Ltd, Astley House, 33 Notting Hill Gate, London W11 3JQ
Tel: +44 (0)20 3675 2450; Fax: +44 (0)20 3675 2451; www.hayhouse.co.uk

Published and distributed in the United States of America by:
Hay House Inc., PO Box 5100, Carlsbad, CA 92018-5100
Tel: (1) 760 431 7695 or (800) 654 5126
Fax: (1) 760 431 6948 or (800) 650 5115; www.hayhouse.com

Published and distributed in Australia by:
Hay House Australia Ltd, 18/36 Ralph St, Alexandria NSW 2015
Tel: (61) 2 9669 4299; Fax: (61) 2 9669 4144; www.hayhouse.com.au

Published and distributed in the Republic of South Africa by:
Hay House SA (Pty) Ltd, PO Box 990, Witkoppen 2068
info@hayhouse.co.za

Published and distributed in India by:
Hay House Publishers India, Muskaan Complex, Plot No. 3, B-2,
Vasant Kunj, New Delhi 110 070
Tel: (91) 11 4176 1620; Fax: (91) 11 4176 1630; www.hayhouse.co.in

Distributed in Canada by:
Raincoast Books, 2440 Viking Way, Richmond, B.C. V6V 1N2
Tel: (1) 604 448 7100; Fax: (1) 604 270 7161; www.raincoast.com

Text © Kyle Gray, 2015

A catalogue record for this book is available from the British Library.

ISBN: 978-1-78180-472-8

Printed and bound in Great Britain by TJ International Ltd, Padstow, Cornwall

To the Divine Mother and her angels
She has many names and many faces,
but her love always lies within the depths of our heart,
waiting for us to arrive.

'If you knew Who walks on the way you have chosen, fear would be impossible.'

A Course in Miracles (Text 18, Chapter 3, Verse 2)

CONTENTS

FOREWORD

As a spiritual teacher I've witnessed countless people crack open to their inner awareness and personal growth. As a spiritual student, I, too, have been on this same journey, one day at a time releasing the blocks to the presence of love within me. When we become spiritual students we arrive seeking happiness, abundance, serenity and – most of all – freedom. We show up willing to do whatever it will take to release ourselves from the bondage of fear. In time, after countless prayers, workshops, counselling sessions, yoga classes, self-help books and silent retreats we come to accept that the freedom we so desperately seek can only come from one radical act: forgiveness.

At first, forgiveness can seem baffling. How can a victim of domestic violence forgive their abuser? Or how can a husband forgive his wife for cheating? Or how can someone who lost a loved one during a terrorist attack forgive that senselessly violent crime? But the 'how' is not important. All that is required is the willingness to forgive.

The moment we become willing to forgive, an invisible force takes over and we receive all the guidance we need. Often this guidance comes in a form we least expect. For me, forgiveness comes through prayer and meditation.

Through my prayer I surrender my false perceptions to the loving care of inner wisdom and guidance. Then I become still and ready to receive. Through meditation I find this stillness and it's in this space that forgiveness is bestowed upon me. Through my meditation practice I have healed all kinds of grievances, from decades of resentment to minor annoyances. Through prayer I surrender to the angels, and through meditation I receive their guidance. Forgiveness is not an act. Forgiveness is a gift bestowed upon us when we become willing to receive it. The moment we surrender, the invisible force of angels leads the way.

My dear friend Kyle Gray knows the powerful force of angels on a very intimate level. For years, Kyle has worked as a medium connecting with the angelic realm to guide people towards the path of forgiveness. Kyle is one of the most authentic spiritual teachers I know. He has enormous integrity. His commitment is not to guide people towards cash, glittering material goods and the power to manifest. His commitment is to guide them towards freedom. Kyle has fearlessly accepted an invitation from the angels. He has chosen to be their divine liaison and to represent them here on Earth.

I can't imagine a hipper representative than Kyle, a tattooed DJ who loves hot yoga. The angels made a smart move choosing Kyle as their partner. His genuine love for life is contagious, and his commitment to serve drives him to deepen his faith daily. We humans are also smart in choosing Kyle as our guide. Kyle is the most awesome spokesperson for the angelic realm. He keeps it real – and his hip presence helps our limited minds resonate with a power beyond our physical site.

In the introduction to this book Kyle speaks of forgiveness and says, 'In this moment angels circle around you, divine *masters in heaven watch down and they offer you a hand – here they stand waiting to lead the way to a newfound freedom, an emotional release and an internal healing that forgiveness offers.'*

What a promise!

Kyle has been given the keys to the kingdom and he has accepted the responsibility of sharing them with you. Through this book, Kyle shares the keys with you so you can open an invisible door to the freedom you desire most. This book is a divine collaboration between Kyle and the angels. Their wisdom will change you forever. Surrender your fears and let the wings of forgiveness lead the way.

Gabrielle Bernstein
New York Times bestselling author of *Miracles Now*

PREFACE

Ever since discovering the power and beauty of angels I've wanted nothing more than to work for them. Very early I felt the inner call, the feeling that I had some sort of higher purpose, but I didn't know what it was or how it would work out. I did know that working in the spiritual field was going to be an emotional journey and that there would be challenges along the way, but I still wasn't prepared for half the experiences I've been through since then.

Time and time again, in almost every session, conversation and workshop I've hosted with angels, there's been one subject that's arisen more than any other. I've never fully understood that subject, or the healing that takes place when it performs its miracles, but there's one thing I do know – it works! I'm talking about forgiveness.

Forgiveness is miraculous. The metaphysical text *A Course in Miracles* defines a miracle as 'a shift of perception' and forgiveness is a moment when we change the way we think about an experience, situation, person or, even more importantly, ourselves. Forgiveness creates a wave of change. It diverts us from anger, resentment and deep-rooted fear and guides us like a pair of wings towards peace, love and calm.

Whenever I have the opportunity to help someone to forgive, I take that opportunity and offer that help. Forgiveness isn't something I can do for someone – I can't even convince them to do it – but what I can do is help them to see the beauty of letting go and feeling free.

Forgiveness is special because it does so much. One of the things I believe it does is create space. It's like a spiritual colonic – it sucks up all of the harsh, toxic, negative and irrational thoughts that bind us to a person, place or situation. It helps us feel lighter and ultimately free.

We can also think of forgiveness as being like polish: it cleans us up and makes us shine. It's a choice we make, a gift we give. Most important of all, it's a gift we give *to ourselves*.

I'm fascinated by the miraculous changes that forgiveness brings. I've witnessed first hand people release weight from their shoulders, cry with joy and let go of what's no longer serving them. I've been the messenger of those on the other side who've asked for forgiveness and I've been the medium for those who need to ask for forgiveness from up above.

Right this moment angels are circling around you and divine masters in heaven are looking down and waiting to lead you to the release, healing and transformation that forgiveness offers. Join us now as we go into the depths of your heart and let this phenomenal miracle work its magic on you!

PROLOGUE

Forgiveness is possible for anyone. I'll never forget the time I came to that realization. It was a Saturday afternoon, the sun was splitting through the clouds and the sky was an icy blue. It was spring and I had a spring in my step. I was on my way to do what I loved: speak to angels and share their love with people. I had three clients booked that day, as I don't like to overdo things and especially at the weekend I like to take some time to myself.

My office is in the centre of Glasgow, adjacent to the central station. Even though it's in the middle of a busy city, a certain peace fills my workspace. More than 20 people come to see me on a weekly basis and at least half of those who visit comment on the peacefulness of the space. I have two altars set up by the windows. One is dedicated to the divine feminine and the other to the divine masculine. A sense of balance is important to me and I like to acknowledge both our Mother and Father, Goddess and God.

That day, I found a woman standing by my door. She was a slender strawberry blonde who looked to be in her early 40s. I wasn't expecting anyone at that time, so, slightly confused, I said, 'Hello, are you waiting to see me?'

She said, 'If you're Kyle, then yes!'

I told her to come back at her appointed time, as I had to set up my office first. But to my surprise, she said, 'Can you just see me now, please? It's really important that I speak to you. I don't know how long I have.'

She looked so serious that I knew she was for real.

'Give me five minutes,' I said.

I went into my office, turned on the heaters and lit the candles as quickly as I could. Closing my eyes in a silent prayer, I called on my angels and thanked them for surrounding me in their protective light. Then I welcomed in the woman, who introduced herself as Rose.

I invited her to take a seat at my desk, where I had my angel cards waiting for our session to begin, and told her that I'd promise her one thing and one thing only: honesty.

'Thank you for doing this,' she said, 'and I have one request before we begin: I don't want to know if there are any spirits in the room. Angels are fine, but I don't want to hear from anyone else who's possibly with me.'

Feeling confused but wanting to honour her wishes, I said, 'I'll try my best, but as you may know, that's generally how I obtain my information about your life and world.'

I instructed her to place her hands on top of the angel cards and I placed my hands on top of hers. We both closed our eyes.

I said, 'Begin to think about anything you'd like to speak about today – anything you'd like your angels to guide you on.'

At that moment I was taken on a whirlwind experience. I saw Rose sitting in the high court, up for trial. Every hair on my body stood on end as I looked at her there in the dock. In my mind, I said, 'Thank you, angels, for giving me the full picture. I want to help her.'

Instantly I was shown Rose fighting a grown man about six feet tall. He was big, strong and not afraid to use his hands. Then I felt as if I was being stabbed in the gut. I gasped, opened my eyes and looked down at my hands. They were covered in blood.

In shock, I whispered, 'Someone's been killed. In fact, I think they were murdered.'

'I wouldn't say "murdered",' Rose replied calmly. 'I strongly believe that's the wrong word. I had to fight for my family – I couldn't let him hurt us anymore.'

I was beginning to get the gist of what was going on. My hands weren't really covered in blood, but my psychic impressions had made it look that way so that I could begin to understand what had happened. And there, right beside Rose, was the six-foot man, in spirit, saying, 'I just want her to know that I forgive her and I want her to forgive me.'

'Whoah,' I said out loud, 'everyone, just give me a minute. I need to get my head around things here.'

It turned out that Rose had suffered years upon years of mental and emotional abuse. Her partner of over 15 years had treated her badly, and her children, too. Finally, she had had enough.

'One of us was going to die that night,' she told me. 'It just happened to be him.'

She hid her partner's body and it was only a few days later, once the adrenaline had faded, that she realized she had to call the police and tell the truth.

She'd come to see me for one thing: forgiveness. And there was her partner's spirit, wanting her to know she was forgiven, but she was still so full of anger, grief and resentment that she didn't want to hear from him. What could I do?

I quietly called on her angels, and as I saw their lights come all around her, I told her that they were there and were wrapping their wings of love around her. Their message came through loud and clear and I shared it with her word for word: 'We angels love you unconditionally and we want you to know the energy you know as God isn't holding any grievances against you. Although on Earth these actions aren't what we would choose, and you yourself wish you had done things differently, you will get to heaven one day. But first you must complete your journey on Earth.'

I explained to Rose that the past was over and we couldn't change it, but it was what we did in the present that was important.

'You're forgiven,' I told her, 'but you must forgive yourself.'

I encouraged her to forgive herself for her actions and for what she felt she'd put her family through. Not only that, she had to forgive her partner – even if that was going to take some time.

No matter what she'd been through, no matter how much she felt like a victim, it was time to surrender it all and move forwards. In order to have any peace in this life, she needed to release the toxicity and resentful thoughts she was holding about her past and present.

The whole time I was speaking, she sat there crying her heart out. Angels were there trying to comfort her and offer support, and I knew it was important not to judge her. I was there to be a light, to share light and help her to see it. Although her actions would unfortunately lead to her imprisonment, I knew deep in my heart that she could make peace with her life if she could just forgive.

She promised me that she'd work on it every day.

It turned out that she was going to the high court for trial the following week, just as I'd seen in my vision. Although I hadn't seen what her fate was, I was honest and told her that, because of her decision to hide her partner's body, I was certain she'd have to serve some time in prison. That didn't seem to bother her, though. What she was really frightened of was having committed the ultimate sin. She didn't want to go to hell – and I was glad to tell her that would not be the case.

Before I wrapped up the session, I said a prayer with Rose and invited the angels of forgiveness to surround her. I also welcomed in the archangels of justice, Raguel and Zadkiel, and thanked them for helping the trial be fair to everyone.

I knew then that my work was done – I'd done my best and even though Rose wasn't open to hearing her partner's message of forgiveness, that message had been delivered anyway through the angels. She knew she wasn't going to hell and by sharing the truth that heaven awaits us all, I'd been able to help create a light in her life again.

What I was most amazed by in this case was seeing the soul of a man who'd brought fear and violence to his family when he was on Earth come through and tell his killer that he forgave her and was seeking her forgiveness – not because it would make him feel better, but because it would help her.

To this day I believe there's more to forgiveness than we realize. It's not always about what we can get from it, but about what we can *give*. *A Course in Miracles* says, 'It is your forgiveness that will bring the world of darkness to the light.' And I believe that to be true.

Chapter 1
WHAT IS FORGIVENESS?

*'Forgiveness stands between illusions and the truth;
between the world you see and that which lies beyond;
between the hell of guilt and heaven's gate.'*
A COURSE IN MIRACLES, LESSON 134

My spiritual introduction to forgiveness took place when I got an angel card deck for my 15th birthday. For those of you who don't know what angel cards are, they are an oracle tool. Each deck contains around 44 cards and each of the cards has a picture of an angel, a message and a keyword. There in those lovely picture cards I learned that forgiveness was powerful and that if we were able to release something that was holding us back, then the most amazing miracles could take place.

The truth is, though, that even though I was introduced to forgiveness in that context very early on in my journey, I still never really knew what it meant to forgive.

When I think back over my life, I suppose the first time I really encountered forgiveness – and unforgiving thoughts – was at school. I remember the trivial disagreements that would happen during playtime, and I especially remember what it was like to feel hurt and let down, as I was a super-sensitive kid.

I'll never forget when one of my best friends started hanging around with someone who was much cooler than me. The two of them excluded me from their trips to the swimming baths or the ice rink after school and finally decided that they weren't speaking to me anymore. For weeks, every time I tried to speak to them, share my snack or show them something I found cool, they'd look in the other direction. It broke my heart.

I remember consulting my mother about this silent treatment and she suggested just taking my friend to one side, away from everyone else, explaining that I appreciated his friendship and suggesting that all of us hang out together so no one felt left out.

I tried this and I'll never forget what happened next. In a complete tantrum, the boy started shouting and screaming at me in the middle of the playground: 'Don't ever speak to me again – I don't want to even *look* at you! I absolutely despise you!'

Not knowing what to say, I just walked away.

Later that night, in tears, I had to ask my mum, 'What does "despise" mean?'

My mum is a very aware mum. I've always called her 'unconsciously conscious', because her intuition and mother's instinct have helped me probably every day of my life. She reminded me that she loved me very much, that I was 'a very special boy' and that I would have plenty of other people to hang around with.

Even though she was right, part of me was left wounded by that experience. All through my school years I just wanted to be accepted. I craved other kids' attention and would do anything to be accepted by them, but for some reason I just kept being left out time and time again.

When I look back now, I suppose a part of me believed that my former friend was right: I wasn't cool enough. In fact, I was despicable. Internally, this opened a can of worms and in many ways challenged me socially and challenged my other friendships, too.

All I wanted was to be forgiven, but I didn't even know what I needed to be forgiven *for*. What part of me was unacceptable?

Like me, there's a great chance that you've searched for forgiveness at some point in your life and there's an even greater chance that you've wanted to feel accepted. We both know what it feels like to be alone, lost and wounded. We know what it's like to try to overcome these feelings and search for some sort of relief and healing.

We're searching because we've the feeling that there's something missing in us, that we're inadequate, or, even worse, we've been *told* we're inadequate! So we go through life feeling that way and not only having challenges with others but also challenges with ourselves. We may search for answers in the world of spirituality, maybe trying hypnotherapy, Reiki, prayer, meditation – even angels.

If you've been searching, if you're looking for relief, you've come to the right place. I don't say that out of ego because there's something 'special' in this book, but more because I've walked – and am still walking – the path of forgiveness. I don't come to you as a teacher, nor do I come to you as some kind of higher being – I'm offering what I've learned as your friend.

You Can Study How to Create Miracles? *Yep!*

As I mentioned earlier, the first time I came across forgiveness in a spiritual sense was through an angel card deck. I remember that when I learned to use these cards, instinctively

I would tell people, 'You need to learn how to forgive yourself.' Even though I was only around 15 or 16 at the time, this guidance seemed to be spot on for everyone who picked the 'Forgiveness' card. To this day I still use that deck and this is the card I think of as the most challenging and healing of all.

It was through this card deck that I began to learn about angels. I discovered they could help us if we called upon them and from very early on in my angelic career I learned that they could help people with forgiveness, whether it was for themselves or others. I realized that when called upon, these amazing beings would guide those who needed forgiveness to change and heal their life.

While on my angel journey, I became fascinated by all the different spiritual authors out there and in particular Doreen Virtue. It was in her book *The Lightworker's Way* that I first came across *A Course in Miracles*. Doreen's journey in *The Lightworker's Way* has been an inspirational one for me, in particular how she healed herself of food addictions and transformed her overweight self – something that I, too, have done.

When I read that Doreen was a student of *A Course in Miracles*, I asked my mum if she would get me a copy and my beautiful mother gave me a hardback copy for Christmas that year. I was thrilled. I thought I was going to experience real miracles like the ones you read about in *Autobiography of a Yogi* by Paramahansa Yogananda, where gurus manifest gold, flowers and perfumed oils out of thin air.

A Course in Miracles is a metaphysical channelled text. Its scribe was a lady called Helen Schucman, who was a psychologist. It came to her via an 'Inner Voice' that she could only describe as 'Jesus'. She put down all of the information she heard on a journey that lasted over seven years.

The *Course* is written in Christian, almost biblical, format, but is a non-religious text. The book has a blue cover with gold writing on the front and is separated into five sections. The first is the text, the next is a workbook of 365 lessons (this is the actual course), then come a manual for teachers, a section clarifying terms and finally some supplements.

When it first landed in my hands over a decade ago I had absolutely no clue where to start with it. The text spoke in a way that was difficult to understand – any part I tried to read went right over my head, and this continued for some time. Eventually, I put the *Course* on my bookshelf and it lay there for some years.

It was strange, though. Even though the *Course* didn't make sense to me I just knew that there was a way of understanding it and that one day it *would* make sense.

It was only five years later that I really began to relate to it and understand what it was teaching me. The breakthrough came when I realized that there was a workbook in the course for a reason and that if I started to work my way through it while reading the text, eventually it would begin to make sense to me. To my pleasant surprise, it did! Now, thanks also to authors and speakers such as Marianne Williamson, Gabrielle Bernstein and my dear friend Robert Holden, the *Course* has become a huge part of my life.

In my eyes, *A Course in Miracles* is a course in forgiveness. It's a 365-day workbook that helps us see the world differently. In fact, it's a manual for changing the way we think.

Its main teaching is very simple: 'Only love is real.' Anything that's not love is 'an illusion'. Basically, fear, pain, hurt, defensiveness and so on are all just illusions – challenges that will disappear if we can 'correct' our way of thinking (and acting) to that of love.

A *Course in Miracles* has become my daily spiritual practice and it has helped me to understand the dynamics of forgiveness. Forgiveness isn't just the act of telling someone (or yourself) that they are forgiven – it's a deeply profound acceptance that love is all there is.

Miracles Explained

Through the study of *A Course in Miracles* I've learned so much about myself, but not only that, I've created a stronger bond with my guardian angels and Creator. Basically, the *Course* reintroduced me to God.

I'm not going to lie – for many years the word 'God' was a complete turn-off for me. That was probably because, like many of you I'm sure, I'd had my challenges with religion and religious people. The God I initially learned about in Sunday school wasn't a God of love but more a God of fear. I was told from very early on that if you didn't ask God for forgiveness for your sins, you'd go straight to hell. Brilliant.

For years I used the word 'universe' or 'source' to replace the word 'God' because there was a part of me that didn't want to be put into the same category as a 'religious' person. But that's just perception, too. Through the changing – and healing – of my perception, I've come to realize that God *is* the universe – not an old man with a stick and not an energy that's cruel. Just as Reverend Run says at the end of his reality TV show, 'God is love.'

When we realize that God isn't cruel or judgemental, and that we're not sinners, we're not going to hell and there's a flow of life wanting to support us in every way possible, our relationship with God will change.

In the *Course* God is referred to as 'He' and to make things easier as I share what I've learned, I'll do the same. But the truth is God is 'He' and 'She' – a divine balance. God is in everyone we meet and God is in us. God is a universal life-force that is everything that is and ever will be.

The *Course* teaches that we are all the 'Son of God' and even though that's a masculine term, in my view it means we're all equal. It reminds us that no person is greater or more gifted than the next, that in fact we're all brothers and sisters on this planet and we're all just as special in the eyes of God.

In addition it helps us to see that our true teacher isn't outside ourselves but, in fact, within. It helps us to reach that state of silence where we can listen to that inner teacher and everything it has to offer us.

The *Course* also teaches that in life there are only ever two states of being: love and fear. When we're in a state of love, we only see and experience love, we totally surrender to the moment we're in, we trust in God and His holy angels and we allow that life-force energy to guide us forwards.

When we're in a state of fear, our perceptions become cloudy and we lack trust. We begin to expect or prepare for the worst and we can't see our own light or that of others. We're caught up in anger, frustration, unhappiness, cynicism and everything else that's not completely loving and accepting.

I'm grateful for the times when I've been in a state of fear because they've been opportunities to remember to focus on love and ultimately to *be* love. The truth is that when we're in a state of fear, we're basically having a nightmare. It's not actually real, because our whole being is love. It's literally divine. But in that moment of fear, we've forgotten about our divinity. However, we can quickly reclaim that divinity by remembering that only love is real!

Returning to Wholeness

We're either ready to return to wholeness or we're on our journey there. What angels have taught me is that we're *already* whole. Our soul is divine light, and that light can be muted in a physical sense, but on a spiritual level it's always shining.

The stars can't shine without the darkness and there's a great chance you've encountered that darkness already, so think of it this way: you're already shining. You're a star, a figment of divine light in the universe, and the beauty of it is that your guardian angels can see it.

You're already whole on the inside, you just need to get your mind and physical body around that idea. When you do, you'll be a walking miracle. As a miracle is a shift of perception, you can dedicate every day of your life to miracles. In fact you're already creating them. The fact that you're here now, with me and in the presence of your guardian angel, shows that you're shifting your way of thinking and preparing yourself for great blessings.

The 'F' Word: 'Forgiveness'

For me, forgiveness has become more than what I learned from my childhood experiences. It isn't just an act or something to say, it isn't a state of mind or a way of thinking, it's a state of being, it's a shift of perception, it's the remembering of love and the eradication of limiting fear-based thoughts and emotions. Forgiveness is a gift we give to ourselves. It removes the blindfold that stops us from seeing love.

In the first section of *A Course in Miracles* there's a list called 'The Principles of Miracles' and I read it all the time. The principles have provided a much-needed source of inspiration to me countless times in my life. While writing this book I decided to create my own principles and they're all about forgiveness. I wrote them while on a road trip with my friends – we were going to Alton Towers, the theme park in Staffordshire, for a day, expressing our inner children with bucketloads of giggles and laughter.

Take some time to study these principles and read them through.

The Principles of Forgiveness

Forgiveness is a deeply profound acceptance of our holiness.

Forgiveness is the total acceptance that we are all equal.

Forgiveness is honouring the divine in others and ourselves.

Forgiveness is the moment we step back into our true self.

Forgiveness is the moment we let love be our source of power.

Forgiveness is the welcome home to peace.

Forgiveness is the awakening of our inner vision.

Forgiveness is a celebration – the angels dance with joy.

Forgiveness is remembering our innocence.

Forgiveness is loving ourselves enough not to accept bad behaviour.

Forgiveness is when someone else's errors no longer affect our happiness.

Forgiveness is the opening to a love that's ever-present.

Forgiveness digests toxicity and initiates healing.

Forgiveness is the remembering that we can never really be hurt, for nothing can tarnish our soul.

Are you ready and willing to forgive?

What Does Forgiveness Mean to You?

In order to shift your perception and allow the miracle of forgiveness to unfold in your life it's really important to spend some time figuring out what forgiveness means to you. If you have a journal it would be perfect to use it for this exercise so you can keep it to look back on, but pen and paper will suffice.

- ✧ Write at the top of the page: 'What does forgiveness mean to me?'
- ✧ Then in the space of 5–10 minutes, write down words, sentences and feelings that will help you uncover what forgiveness means to you. The principles above may help you.

When you've dug into your instinctive feelings about the word 'forgiveness', you'll understand how it can impact your life.

You can make this exercise even better if you have a partner. You sit facing each other and your partner asks you over and over, 'What does forgiveness mean to you?' Each time you answer with something new. This way, without too much thinking you bring to light your deepest feelings about this miraculous shift in perception. Then swap over: you do the asking and your partner reveals their views.

Here's a prayer based on one in *A Course in Miracles*, which I've written for you to invoke the vision and mindset of forgiveness so that you can begin to incorporate this state of being into your daily life and live a life that is fuelled by love.

> 'Dear God, Universal Life-Force and Creator,
> I am like you. No cruelty abides in me, for there is none in you.
> Your peace belongs to me. I bless the world with the peace I have received from you alone.

I choose today and for the highest good to make the choice for all of humanity, knowing we are one with you. I bring them your salvation as I have received it now. And I give thanks for them, for within them I see and recognize your light and in them I find your peace. Holy are we because your holiness has set us free. For freedom, I am thankful.

I awaken the vision of forgiveness. I forgive and I am forgiven.

And so it is.'

Chapter 2
A HOLY ENCOUNTER

*'Angels listen when she speaks: She's my
delight, all mankind's wonder...'*
<small>JOHN WILMOT ROCHESTER</small>

I never knew I was going to write a book on forgiveness. The truth is, a part of me didn't feel qualified. Forgiveness is deep. It's a healing acceptance that doesn't only affect our life but travels deep into our soul. How could I write about that? But then I had a holy encounter.

Ever since I'd read the book *The Da Vinci Code* in my teenage years I'd been fascinated by Mary Magdalene. To be honest, before that I'd never heard much about her other than the stories you'd hear about 'Jesus's friend, Mary' at Sunday school.

When you ask most people what they know about Mary Magdalene, there's a great chance that they'll turn around and say she was a prostitute. Rumours spread that she was the lowest of the low in society – a complete sinner who was forgiven by the Lord. As such, today she's a powerful symbol of redemption for many. But it's almost as if she was called a prostitute because over the years people speculated that Jesus may have had a relationship with her. I suppose this caused some uproar in-house, especially when having relations was frowned upon or even seen as 'unholy'. Although years later the Church apologized and made her into a saint, to this day many remember her as a whore, which ultimately is not the truth.

Someone literally got their stories mixed up – in fact, it was Pope Gregory I in the sixth century. He made the assumption that the Mary who washed the feet of Jesus with her hair was Mary Magdalene, when it was, in fact, Mary the sister of Martha. Even so, I can't look at that Mary in a negative light. Yes, she was a prostitute, but she was trying to survive with the best knowledge she had at the time. We can only send her love.

The Gal Who Knows Forgiveness

Since learning about Mary Magdalene all those years ago, whenever I thought of her, I always felt to offer forgiveness would be her role. Maybe that was because her memory had been tarnished in such a horrible way and deep down I'd always known her soul held no grievances but existed in a space of eternal love.

I've always had her high on my spiritual prayers list. In fact a while back I had her portrait tattooed onto my arm. She's a youthful woman with large eyes veiled by a reversed triangle, acknowledging the divine feminine. At her heart centre she holds a cup, representing the Holy Grail and the fact that women are the vessels of life. Below the cup there is a rose, representing unconditional love.

Back when I was around 20, I decided to look into the history of Mary Magdalene to really get to know her background. I soon learned that she had a gospel and I went straight out to get a copy. Sure I read it, but, being a young man, life got in the way and I never really continued my study of Mary. I just went on believing that she was a spiritual guide to anyone who called on her.

Initiation

My relationship with Mary Magdalene really opened up when I least expected it. In fact, it was just this year and God knows I wasn't prepared for what happened. It was when I was speaking at one of Hay House's amazing events, 'I Can Do It: Ignite' in London, that I believe some sort of divine initiation took place.

One of the other speakers was Meggan Watterson. Meggan is a self-confessed 'theologian in hot pants' and she specializes in the divine feminine. Her book, *Reveal*, is a manual for getting spiritually naked. Everyone had been telling me I was going to absolutely love her, but whenever I hear people say that I always keep an open mind and decide for myself.

My friend Hollie Holden invited me to sit with her for Meggan's talk. Sitting on the right-hand side of the auditorium, second row from the front, I was excited to see Meggan take to the stage.

As soon as she came out, I was hooked. It was as if there was a golden light burning brightly around her. She was wearing an orange dress which sculpted beautifully to her figure. Not only that, she was funny – I was soon laughing at her dry humour and I could feel that there was something deeply healing happening to my soul.

During her talk Meggan told us that we were the truth we were all looking for. That within us all was a divine soul voice that was connected to the eternal love source that had created us. This was an exquisite reminder that I was divine and I so needed to hear it.

What I loved even more was that Meggan spoke about the Indian goddess Kali and then went on to talk about my favourite woman: Mary Magdalene. What was weird was that I had both of these figures tattooed on me. I was getting really excited by now. I was so impressed by the fact that this woman had put herself on stage in such a loving and vulnerable way – she was encouraging us all to strip our spirituality back to basics.

Meggan spoke wholeheartedly about why she was interested in the divine feminine, but made it clear that she wasn't there to create feminists, rather to bring balance to how we all see the divine. It was then that she did something that I wasn't prepared for: she announced that she was going to share a passage from a second-century Gnostic text known as 'Thunder Perfect Mind'.

Standing centre stage, she opened her arms, palms facing forwards, looked into the air and began to recite:

'I am the first and the last.
I am the honoured and the scorned.
I am the whore and the holy one.
I am the wife and the virgin.
I am the mother and the daughter.
I am a barren woman who has many children.
I have had many weddings,
And have taken no husband.
I am the silence that is incomprehensible
And insight whose memory is great.
I am the voice whose sounds are many.
I am the utterance of my own name.
Why have you hated me in your counsels?
I am the lamp of the heart.'

Whatever happened in that instant, it felt so divine and holy. My clairvoyant vision opened and I could see a wave flowing towards the whole audience. It was ruby red and it was coming at me like a tsunami. I was apprehensive, but I knew I wanted it to wash over me.

As it hit me, it took my breath away. I fell back into my chair and lost track of what was happening, never mind where I was. I haven't a clue what was said in the last few minutes of Meggan's talk. All I remember is an immense love. It felt as if my heart had cracked open. If there had been padlocks holding it closed, they were there no more. I felt miraculously held and my vision opened up and I saw angels everywhere. I turned and looked at the rest of the audience. I wish they could have seen what I was seeing: divine angels of love were gathered all around us, ensuring our souls were soaking up the support they needed.

In the midst of all this, I suddenly remembered I was due to be interviewed by a newspaper and then go on stage to speak for an hour. I needed to get myself together. I quietly crept out of the hall and went to the bathroom. I had to lock myself in a cubicle for a few moments to get my head around what just had happened to my soul.

The voice of 'Thunder Perfect Mind' felt like that of Mary Magdalene. It seemed to me that Meggan had just channelled her. Not only that, although there were probably over 500 people in the hall that day, I felt as though whatever it was had been aimed directly at me.

'What the heck was that?' I said to myself.

The voice of Kamael, my guardian angel, replied, 'All will soon be revealed.'

I said a prayer to ground myself and caught my breath for a few moments. I needed to remember what I was here to share.

As Hay House publicist Ruth and I were on our way to meet the journalist for the interview, I said to her, 'Oh my *God* – I *love* Meggan Watterson. I need to meet her this weekend!'

Ruth laughed and said, 'She's quite amazing, eh?'

'Yeah – she just channelled some Goddess energy there and I'm blown away. Will she be here later?'

'I think she's going back to the hotel now.'

That wasn't what I was hoping to hear, but in my heart I said, 'Angels, thank you for organizing a meeting with Meggan later so we can connect,' and I surrendered to the moment.

After my interview (which went really well), I went backstage and prepared to close the Saturday afternoon programme. I was really looking forward to sharing my message about the angels and the power of prayer.

I never really know what to say at these events, or shall I say I never come overly prepared because I like to share from the heart centre – to say whatever I'm inspired to say at the time. In fact, what I always do is write a prayer to support my talk in my journal and then, if I remember, I open up the talk with the prayer. That's what I did on this occasion. And, as I gazed into the audience, about to start my prayer, I noticed Meggan Watterson was sitting where I'd been sitting before. Now *she* was watching *me*…

I read my prayer, which I will share with you now:

Dear angels,

I thank you for allowing me to be a voice – your voice – in helping others discover their natural gifts and talents. Thank you for guiding me in what to say, how to say it and how to guide others. I am overjoyed to work with you in the light of God's grace and take this extra opportunity to share my gratitude with you. I love how we're on the same team and I love how we can help people keep it real together. You are my guides, I am your biggest fan and I know that you are mine. Let's rock it, guys – I love you.

And so it is!'

The audience smiled and I began to share my story for what seemed like three minutes but was actually an hour. I talked directly to the audience, but I couldn't help looking over at Meggan now and then – she was pulling me in. Nothing like this had ever happened before – what was going on?

I wrapped up and did my book signing as normal, then made my way back to the hotel. Jessica, Hay House's events coordinator, invited me to join her for dinner, which was great.

To my surprise and delight, when I got to the restaurant, sitting at the table were Jessica, Hay House's amazing publicity director Jo Burgess and … Meggan.

Before I could even say anything, Meggan was telling me that she'd loved my talk. I was flabbergasted – I needed to tell her everything.

That whole night just blew me away. Meggan and I chatted about Mary Magdalene and Kali and shared our love for angels and prayer. It was simply amazing. I truly felt that I'd met my sister, new best friend and soul buddy all at the same time. And Meggan's words from 'Thunder Perfect Mind' had awakened a need in me to go back home and dig out all my Mary Magdalene texts and do a bit of studying – I felt that there was something there for me to discover.

When I finally headed home, I took Meggan's book with me. I really loved its very honest message about being spiritually vulnerable and naked. In fact, I decided that in order to be spiritually naked I needed to get physically naked, too. I took off all my clothes and got into a nice warm bath with Meggan's book.

I was reading away and really enjoying it when I started to drift away. I put the book down and lay back in the bath. Closing my eyes, I moved into a deep, trance-like state.

All of a sudden I found myself in a deep, red crystal cave. There were ruby-like crystals everywhere, glistening in the light. Though I say 'light', the cave was actually in darkness. It was nothing negative – more as if it was night-time.

Suddenly there was a female figure in front of me, gazing into my eyes. Her own were dark brown, like chocolate. Her heart-shaped face was beautiful and her cheekbones were high. Her hair was wrapped in a red veil, but I could see it tumbling out from underneath. She was cloaked in red – a red I can only describe as 'blazing'.

'I am here to help you with the book on forgiveness.'

I heard the words loud and clear. They were direct and simple and I knew I needed to take note of them.

I asked out loud, 'Forgiveness? Wait – where am I?'

'You are in the cave of your heart. I will meet you here.'

I realized this was a holy encounter with Mary Magdalene. And then I woke up.

For the rest of the evening a feeling of bliss just washed over me. It was amazing, but I knew that I'd been given a mission from heaven and I had to listen to the guidance. I began to make notes in my journal and record everything I felt inspired by.

The Gnostic Gospels

As I lay in bed that night, the realization came over me that Mary Magdalene hadn't only visited me when I was in the bath, she'd come to me that day at 'Ignite', too. She'd been the red wave initiated by Meggan – it had been her light that had washed over me. It was as if angels and ascended masters had orchestrated events so that I would be at that talk and be invited to see that Mary Magdalene was there to support the work I was doing. In fact, I felt that she was going to become the spirit guide of the whole project.

The next day I went to my office and began looking through every spiritual book I had on saints, ascended masters, Jesus and the Holy Grail in the hope I would find some more information about her. I also took out my Gnostic Gospels to find her message.

The Gnostic Gospels are a collection of over 50 texts that are based upon the teachings of many spiritual leaders. They were written between the second and fourth centuries after Jesus's death. 'Gnostic' comes from the Greek word *gnosis*, which means 'knowledge' and can be interpreted as 'enlightenment', or what I like to call divine guidance.

The Gnostic Gospels aren't part of the standard canon known as the New Testament. They offer a new way of thinking (well, not that new really), an alternative view of the teachings of Jesus. What has impressed me is the fact that in them, women are given a voice, and source energy is recognized as 'Mother–Father'. This adds a whole new dimension to the message. I immersed myself in 'The Gospel of Mary Magdalene' and the experience was heartwarming and enlightening.

Over the course of my study of this insightful text, I've realized that it's all about the journey of the soul. It's about human beings remembering their spiritual truth and sharing it with the world – just like all the teachings on spiritual growth that I and other people are sharing with the world today.

Pages one to six of the manuscript are missing, so the gospel starts with Chapter 2, a teaching from Jesus:

All natures, all forms, all creatures exist in and with one another, and they will be resolved again into their own roots. For the nature of matter is released into the roots of its nature.

Chapter 2, verses 2–5

Here Jesus is teaching something that sages, yogis and physicists are telling us today: *we are all one*.

He continues when Peter asks him, 'Since you have explained everything to us, tell us one other thing: what is the sin of the world?'

Jesus said:

> *'There is no sin, but it is you who make sin when you do the things that are like the nature of adultery, which is called "sin". That is why Good came into your midst, coming to the good which belongs to every nature, in order to restore it to its root.'*

Chapter 3, verses 3–6

Jesus is sharing a very important piece of information that could have changed Christian ideas on sin entirely if this text had been included in the canon. He's telling us that it is we who create sin – that there are things down here that we may consider wrong, but they're not going to stop us from being Good. I love how he gives 'Good' a capital letter when he's pointing out the most important thing: Good exists within you. It's your nature – it's who you are. This Good is your inner divinity; it's your most Holy self. It's your soul.

The teachings of this gospel are what you've probably known all along and have heard countless times: you are spirit, you have a soul, and it's the part of you that can't be destroyed. Sure you'll make mistakes and, yes, you'll want to change parts of your life, but the truth is the goodness within you can't be removed. It's the part of you that's waiting for your attention – it's waiting to grow and rise with you.

Humanity

The final part of Jesus's teaching before he exits the scene is a huge wake-up call for us all. Whether you believe in the existence of Jesus or not, or even in the validity of this text, it makes no difference, because its words will resonate with your soul if you're ready to undertake the journey of forgiveness.

Before he departs, Jesus says:

'Peace be with you! Bear my peace within yourselves! Beware that no one lead you astray, saying, "Look over here!" or "Look over there!" For the Child of Humanity is within you! Follow it! Those who seek it will find it. Go then and proclaim the good news of the realm. Do not lay down any rules beyond what I determined for you, nor give a law like a lawgiver, lest you be confined by it.'

Chapter 4, verses 2–10

This message had me so excited because here Jesus is teaching us not to let anyone or anything distract us from our goodness. He's encouraging us to stay peaceful and not to let anyone insult us or sidetrack us from our own inner divinity. When he says that the Child of Humanity is within us, what he means is that in truth we are all gentle and kind, because the definition of humanity is benevolence. He encourages us to tell people of their goodness and to share our own goodness with all those around us (the realm), before reminding us not to be restricted by made-up rules or laws that get in the way of our growth. This is so important. If we followed this guidance, maybe forgiveness wouldn't even be an issue. I'll leave you to meditate on that.

Discovering the Magdalene

The introduction to Mary in the gospel had me completely spellbound and confirmed what my intuitive impressions of her were telling me.

It starts with Mary seeing the followers of Jesus saddened because of his crucifixion (or so it seems, though it doesn't actually say that). They appear scared to pass on his words and wisdom. Mary stands up like a leader and says:

> *'Do not weep and be pained, nor doubt, for all his grace will be with you and shelter you. But rather let us praise his greatness, for he has prepared us and made us Humans.'*

The passage continues with true leading and loving authority from Mary:

> *When Mary said this, she turned their heart to the Good, and they began to discuss the words of the saviour.*
> *Chapter 5, verses 9 and 10*

It's clear here that Mary had a divine mission on Earth: she wanted to remind the other followers of Jesus that love was real and that they were human beings. The term 'human beings' is actually an interesting play on words. For me, it refers to spiritual beings walking a human pathway and it seems that Mary was well aware of that fact. How could the others forget so easily? How could they doubt? Fortunately, Mary was there as a channel and a reminder that love existed and they could go forwards on their path.

Powerful Visions

Mary Magdalene reveals in her gospel that she is a powerful visionary. In this day and age we would call it 'clairvoyance', for she saw Jesus after his death. But not only that: she also saw angels!

The story that is told in the Gospel of John confirms in my eyes that not only was Mary human, but she was open to the most spiritual of experiences. It begins with her visiting the tomb of Jesus in the early hours of the morning when it was still dark, only to discover that it had been opened and Jesus was missing. She rushed back to tell Simon Peter and the other disciples and they came running. They didn't know what to do, so they went back to their companions and waited while Mary stayed at the tomb, close to the opening. She was weeping because the Master she loved so much was missing from his place of rest. As she wept, she looked over to where Jesus's burial cloths were lying and his body should have been and saw an angel of pure white sitting where Jesus's head had been and another where his feet had been.

The angels spoke to Mary and asked her why she was so upset. She told them it was because her Master had been taken away. Then she turned around and saw someone else there. She began to ask him if he'd taken her Master. Here's what happens next, directly from the Gospel of John, Chapter 20, verses 16–19:

> 'Mary!' said Jesus. She turned around, and exclaimed in Hebrew: 'Rabboni!' (which is to say, 'Teacher.') 'Do not touch me,' Jesus said; 'for I have not yet ascended to the Father. But go to my brothers, and tell them I am ascending to my Father and their Father, my God and their God.' Mary Magdala went and told the disciples that she had seen the Master, and that he had said this to her.'

It's clear here that Mary Magdalene had a strong spiritual encounter with Jesus, even though at first she didn't recognize him. Maybe this was because he was healed or his spiritual body was somehow different from his physical one. Whatever the case, Mary became the medium of his message and in my eyes that makes her a channel and a visionary who had a purpose to serve and share. She became the Apostle to the Apostles – she put them on their journey by channelling Jesus's love to them. And he came to her first – she was the first person to see him after his resurrection and before he ascended to heaven. It was a very powerful connection.

Mary Gave Betrayal the 'F' Word

Mary told the other disciples that she'd been visited by Jesus and received new information that would help their quest. However, despite sharing what I can only call divine guidance, she was shot down in flames by many of the other disciples. They questioned why she of all people would have received the guidance, rather than any of them.

Mary was initially upset by this experience. She felt betrayed because she'd already guided others to remember the good that was within them. Eventually, however, Levi, who was also known as Matthew, came out in support of her vision.

The impression given by the text is that even though Mary was upset, she didn't hold a grudge, and eventually the disciples went out and shared the 'good news' according to her guidance.

Ascended Master

In my meditations I have come to realize that Mary Magdalene is not only what people would call a saint, she's an ascended master who can be called upon by anyone. She was a spiritual teacher and leader on Earth and she continues in this role on the other side. So, we can all call on her to guide and support us on our journey of forgiveness.

Mary works closely with the angelic realm to bring healing and guidance to all those who really open their heart to her presence. Throughout this book I will share her love and teachings with you all.

Mary has a red aura, but it's not a dense red – it shines and sparkles like a ruby left in the sunlight. When you call upon her, she will bring it to the centre of your being so that she can lovingly guide you from the inside.

Let Mary Magdalene be your guide to forgiveness and let her support you on this journey of freedom and remembering your inner divinity.

Releasing Betrayal, Remembering Good

Like Mary Magdalene, there's probably been a point in your life when you've felt betrayed and let down. There's a great chance that within you somewhere you're giving more energy to that feeling of betrayal than to channelling your inner good. Is there something that's bothering you now or something from your past that you no longer need? Are you giving your past power? Are you adding anger to the betrayal and adding fuel to the fire?

✧ Before moving further into this book, spend some time thinking about areas of your life in which you've experienced betrayal or feel you've been unfairly singled out. Is there a way of thinking differently about them? Can you see the situation in a different light now? Can you choose to remember something good instead or focus on a lighter emotion to remove the karmic pattern that has been created?

✧ Are there parts of your past that you feel need a miracle to resolve? Write in your journal, or just on a piece of paper, all the areas, past and present, in which you are willing to receive support.

✧ Do you still resonate with resentment when you think about these issues or have your feelings become lighter now? Write down your emotions, instincts and feelings.

When you've done this, say this prayer:

'Divine soul, Mary Magdalene,

Thank you for unveiling your ruby light and shining it upon me now.

I welcome with open arms your guidance, support and protection as I undertake this sacred journey.

Thank you for igniting within the cave of my heart a flame of love, a flame that will purify and cleanse all thoughts and memories of fear, anger and anguish.

As the flame burns brightly, I return to love and remember my holiness.

Thank you for helping me to see that I am spirit.

Thank you for helping me to accept love and to perceive forgiveness as it is.

Welcome to my heart, sweet Mary Magdalene. I allow this journey to unfold.

And so it is.'

Chapter 3
ANGELS OF FORGIVENESS

'In this dim world of clouding cares
we rarely know, till 'wildered eyes
see white wings lessening up the skies.
The angels with us unawares.'
GERALD MASSEY, ENGLISH POET

There is a choir of millions of angels that are dedicated to forgiveness. These amazing angels have shown themselves to me clairvoyantly in a number of different ways. One of the most memorable visions included a huge being around seven feet tall, with blue lightning coming from it and four wings on its back!

When we welcome the angels of forgiveness into our life, we are allocated a 'forgiveness angel' who stays with us throughout our journey here on Earth. These angelic presences are dedicated to helping us release the limiting thoughts and beliefs that stand between us and love.

Whenever I think about forgiveness angels, I see in my mind various colours coming through: the healing rays of green, the ruby red of loyalty, the yellow of drive and joy, the blues of healing and communication… Forgiveness angels are here to help us with all of these things and more. They are wonderfully healing beings who desperately want to help us with forgiveness.

I remember, during a private session with a lovely girl in her 30s, seeing an extra angel with her, draped in a beautiful golden robe. The angel was male, with blue eyes, high cheekbones, a square jaw and golden locks – typically angelic. The girl herself was holding a lot of frustration and unforgiving thoughts towards herself, others and even God. She just felt so helpless and lost. Every relationship in her life had fallen apart. She had had problems with her parents, her previous partners had cheated on her and someone she'd trusted had borrowed money and never given it back. She was in an unhappy place in her career and her body felt more like a prison that the home of her soul. She was at the end of her tether and had come to me as a last resort.

I remember during the course of our session together acknowledging all the events that had happened and witnessing all the anger, frustration and hidden emotions rising to the surface – she was ready to blow.

At that moment the golden-robed angel stepped forwards and wrapped his wings around her. As he did so, she began to cry and said, 'I can feel a warmth coming over me right now.'

'There's a beautiful angel wrapping his wings around you,' I told her. 'He's here to help heal you and lead you to happiness.'

I just knew that this was the reason why the angel was there. This instinctive knowing is common with angels – they just plant their messages in your mind. Whether you call yourself psychic or not, the spark of their presence ignites an inner awareness.

As the girl began to sob, letting go of the pain that she'd held in for weeks, months and even years, I could see that a true sense of relief was washing over her. I remember sitting there with her in my office, holding her hand as she released all her anger and frustration. The angel held his wings around her, the angel cards were spread in front of us and I told her she was in a safe place.

When she finally managed to breathe a sigh of relief, I asked her, 'Where do you go from here? What's your instinctive guidance?'

I'll never forget what happened next as long as I live.

Taking another deep breath, she said, 'I'm ready to forgive!'

At that moment the angel began to weep, too. It was so moving to see this angel of pure light weeping tears of joy. He revealed to me that he was an angel of forgiveness and had been with this girl the whole time in complete faith that she would be ready to forgive one day.

The angels of forgiveness cannot press us or tell us what to do, but they can stand by in hope and faith that we will eventually reach our maximum potential. The angel who came forth in this story was about to begin his sacred mission of leading this girl to the freedom that forgiveness brings.

You can welcome the angels of forgiveness into your life simply by saying this affirmative angel prayer:

'Thank you, angels, for helping me to understand the miracle of forgiveness.'

Angels always want to help us forgive because they know that when this happens, our whole life refocuses on love.

One thing I've noticed is that a complete restoration of innocence comes to us when we forgive – it's as if we become children again and begin once more to see the wonders of life. You'll know, especially if you have children in your life, that these small teachers are very quick to forgive and move on from a situation and they're widely accepting little beings.

Of course as we grow older we learn how to hold grudges and harbour pain, but if you want my opinion on that, I think it's completely abnormal. Forgiveness should be second nature, an automatic response, because it relieves us of a burden.

While at an Angel Congress weekend at Basel once, I presented a one-day workshop on forgiveness for a small group. There were around 30 of us and it was a beautiful afternoon. During the workshop, I told everyone that because they'd consciously chosen to be on a forgiveness workshop, the angels of forgiveness would be drawing close and would give them a sign of their presence. Just a week later I received this letter from a girl called Romy, who had been on the course:

Dear Kyle,

I'd like to share with you something that happened just after your wonderful 'forgiveness workshop' in Basel.

Just a day afterwards I was playing on my bed with my third child, Valentin, who is two and a half years old. Suddenly he took my notebook from the workshop, which was lying on my bed. In fact, the notebook was quite empty, as most of the information I had saved in my heart. My son said, in a determined way, 'Mommy, I read to you!' He then proceeded to open my notebook and pretended to read to me. He pointed to the blank white sheets of paper and said in Swiss-German, 'Ängeli, Ängeli, Ängeli ...' which means 'Angels, angels, angels.'

I was so astonished, happy and grateful at the same time. I had never told him about angels before. I'd kept my connections inside me, but now I know it's time to share my truth and that I'm on my divine path. Thank you.

Blessings,

Romy

Angels never cease to amaze me. These powerful beings are just waiting for any opportunity to remind us of their wonderful presence. In this case Romy's son became an 'unconsciously conscious' messenger to her and reminded her that her journey of forgiveness with the angels was really opening up and that they were real and present in her life. I trust that she will now begin to follow this pathway with unwavering faith, thanks to this amazing holy encounter.

My own forgiveness angel came to me during my Reiki Master-Teacher attunement on 13 January 2013. This took place at the house of Roisin, my Reiki Master, in Drymen, near Loch Lomond, 30 minutes from Glasgow. As she attuned me to the Master level of this amazingly powerful healing technique, I had a vision of a bright blue angel with a face made of stars like the night sky moving towards me. He was beautiful and otherworldly. In my mind I heard the name 'Joel' and saw it spelled out.

I remember telling Roisin about the new angel I'd encountered during the experience. It turned out that she'd felt that there had been angels all around us.

The reason Joel came to me at that time was because I was ready to step even more into the light and transcend the emotions, thoughts and challenges that I'd endured in the past.

Afterwards I looked up the name 'Joel' and found that it was a Hebrew name that could be interpreted as 'The Lord is God', which is quite fitting, don't you think?

Since that experience I've developed my relationship with this angel through my daily forgiveness practice.

Get High Vibe!

To experience your forgiveness angel it's always best to strengthen your spiritual connection and raise your vibration. I know those words sound a little crazy, right? But let me explain it to you.

Everything in the entire universe is energy vibrating at one frequency or another. We've all felt these frequencies – we've probably just called them 'negative' or 'positive' vibes.

For example, you know what it's like to walk into a room and feel that you could cut the atmosphere with a knife. And you know when someone's in a bad mood or having a strop. These are perfect examples of a 'low vibration'.

Now let's talk about the opposite. You know what it's like when you feel happy about something or grateful for a blessing in your life. You know that feeling that comes over you when you remember someone you love or a happy time from your childhood. You know how it feels when you're so happy you want to cry. These are perfect examples of a 'high vibe'. Angels are made of that high-vibrational energy.

In order to develop a relationship with your angels, and your forgiveness angel in particular, you need to learn how to connect with them. To do this, you need to raise your energy.

Ritual to Raise Energy

✧ Begin by thinking about something that you are grateful for in your life.

✧ Smile, feel the warmth of the blessing that's in your mind.

✧ Think about loved ones who make you feel blessed.

✧ Now imagine you are enveloped in golden light.

✧ Say, internally: 'I am enveloped in a golden light of source energy!'

✧ Imagine that there are angels all around you.

✧ See an angel in your mind on your left and your right.

✧   Feel angels behind you, protecting you.

✧   Hear the wings of angels flutter as they float above you.

✧   Then say: 'Thank you, angels, for drawing close and for reminding me of your presence.'

✧   Take a deep breath and trust your angels are close.

Hanging Out with Angels

It takes some time to have a full-on connection with angels, but some of us are blessed to see or feel their presence more than others. I really believe that experiencing angels is down to our commitment and openness. You know your intuition and spiritual senses are like muscles that you don't always use or perhaps haven't ever used. You know what it feels like when you haven't worked out for a while – it's pretty challenging, right? It can be the same with meeting your guides and angels, so before you take further steps, it's important to remember these things take time. Loving yourself throughout your exploration of your angels is absolutely critical. So, if you feel that you're not progressing and you're about to beat yourself up over the situation, or you keep feeling that you aren't as able as others, *stop*. Take time to love yourself and appreciate that these muscles just need some time to grow.

I believe that we already know our angels and when we decide to contact them, it's essentially a remembering process. Taking time to breathe and relax into the experience is the greatest gift we can give ourselves.

Here's a meditation for you. Now, when you practise meditation on your own, there's one tip I suggest: record it!

This means you don't have to open your eyes and look up the next step. Most of us have a free and readily available recording device on our phone. When I need to guide myself into a state of meditation, I just talk myself through the steps and into a state of deep meditative bliss. Are you ready to do the same?

Meeting Your Forgiveness Angel

When you want to meet your forgiveness angel, there really is no wrong way to do it. If you just meditate and go off on your own wee journey, there's a great chance your angelic friend will show up if you invite them. If you need some pointers, though, here are my steps to meeting your forgiveness angel:

✧   Clear the space around you. If you're easily distracted in meditation, remove all potential diversions from your sight and space.

✧   Make sure the room is the right temperature and decide where you will sit to do the practice.

✧   Light some candles to prepare the space and surround yourself with objects that feel loving and spiritual – maybe a photo of a loved one, some crystals and your angel card deck if you have one.

✧   Before closing your eyes, invoke protection through this prayer:

'Thank you, universal life-force and angels, for surrounding me and this space in a light of unconditional love and protection. Thank you for looking after this whole experience and what is learned from it.'

✧   Close your eyes and focus on your breath. You may want to hold your belly to feel the rhythm of your breath and to connect with your body.

✧　Affirm within: 'I am safe! And this experience is safe.'

✧　With your eyes closed, imagine that you are in a beautiful light-filled space. You feel as if you are in a cave of light and you feel so loved.

✧　At the centre of this space, waiting for you, is your angel of forgiveness.

✧　In your mind's eye, become aware of this angel. Are they appearing to you as a man or a woman or a sexless being? Can you hear their voice? Are they speaking to you? Are they giving you their name? Do you recognize them? Do you remember who they are?

✧　Know that you are standing in the cave of your own heart and being blessed by the presence of your forgiveness angel.

✧　Thank your forgiveness angel for revealing to you their name and identity (even if they haven't yet done so). Thank them for giving you any messages you need to know.

✧　Spend time in this space. Trust the conversations that you have with this being. Trust the feelings that move through your body and know you are being guided to remember the light that you are.

✧　Once you feel you have recognized your angel, thank them for sending you reminders of their presence and hug them. Know that they are forever waiting in the cave of your heart.

✧　Make your way back to your body by becoming aware of yourself sitting back where you started. Wiggle your fingers and toes, move your joints and stretch before opening your eyes and coming back to the room.

Archangel Jeremiel

Archangels are like the manager angels of heaven. They oversee the guardian angels and ensure they're fulfilling their duties (which of course they are). These amazing beings are powerful and peaceful warriors who are supporting us with their light. There are probably thousands of archangels out there, but without a doubt some are better known than others. One particular archangel I work with and call on often is Archangel Jeremiel. In my eyes, he is the archangel of forgiveness.

I call Jeremiel 'the miracle worker' because he can help us to understand why it's useful to forgive and how we can make forgiveness possible. I see him in my clairvoyant vision surrounded by pure golden and orange light. Angels always show themselves to us in a way we'll understand and I see Jeremiel as a tall and slender angel with golden skin and golden shoulder-length hair, much like the forgiveness angel I described earlier. His eyes are deep blue and he wears a cloak of wisdom. He carries a torch that shines the light of God's mercy on any situation that requires forgiveness. You'll see his image on the front cover of this book.

'Jeremiel' in Hebrew means 'the mercy of God', and Archangel Jeremiel is the divine spokesperson and representation of God's mercy. The word 'mercy' is powerful because it represents compassion and forgiveness. When it comes to a challenging situation in your life in which forgiveness is needed, you have the choice whether to be merciful or to punish. Mercy is the higher road; it's the choice of love, not only because it's giving someone the gift of forgiveness, but because when you choose to be merciful you no longer hold the toxic thoughts and resentment that can damage you inside.

I recently had a private session with a client who had been having a bumpy relationship. Lauren had kicked her partner out so many times that she'd lost count! After some thought, she'd decided to let him back in 'one final time', but all she'd been doing since was making him suffer. Every little mistake he'd made in the past and every trivial problem in the present were punished. Lauren would shout her head off and become deeply emotional. She couldn't see any way forwards in her relationship – but she couldn't see any way forwards in her life either.

When I invited the angels into the room to help heal this situation, I was made aware that Archangel Jeremiel wanted to bring a message to Lauren. As her guardian angel moved to the side to let the almighty golden archangel step behind her, she reported, 'Every hair on my body is standing on end.' I could see a light of complete healing moving over her. It was magnificent.

This clear and distinctive message followed: 'It is time to stop punishing yourself. Every time you are harmful to your partner, you are harmful to yourself. There is love in your relationship, but you cannot see it because your focus is on pain.'

When I relayed the message verbatim to Lauren, she began to cry as the realization hit her that when she cast up something from the past or pointed out what she didn't like in her partner, it caused her just as much pain and distress as it gave him. I remember her saying, 'I just need to tell him how grateful I am that we have so many happy memories. All I've done is focus on the blips in our relationship.'

We prayed to Jeremiel together and thanked him for sending his wave of light into Lauren's life. In the prayer we gave complete permission to Jeremiel to highlight the pathway to peace and to help Lauren understand what it really meant to forgive in her relationship.

It can be easier for many of us to focus on the past, in particular on the problems we've encountered along the way, than on what we have to be grateful for now, but according to *A Course in Miracles* that's not our real nature. Our true self is always love and as soon as we focus on the pain of a situation we've taken a wrong turn – we've diverted away from our true selves and the gifts the present moment offers.

Lauren e-mailed me a few weeks later and said that her relationship had turned around. When she'd initiated a deep loving talk with her partner, they'd both realized they just needed to forget about their past hang-ups and move on together.

Jeremiel, as his name says, is 'the mercy of God' and he can ignite compassion and forgiveness within us. He can help us to see ourselves in a better light and turn our past fears into present love.

Just like the other archangels, Jeremiel can be with all of us at once. He's not limited by time and space – his energy is ever-present and will come to anyone who calls on him. I've seen him help many people when it comes to the dynamics of forgiveness.

So many of us try to forgive but can't forget. I've found that Archangel Jeremiel can't help us to forget a situation, but he can help us to forget the pain. Through the teachings of this amazing archangel I've learned that we're always whole. Even though we may feel hurt, let down and broken, the truth is we're not. Our soul will always remain completely whole – we just need to allow our physical self to accept that.

Whenever I've called on Jeremiel, he's helped me to see my way forwards. I remember recently when I was feeling really low about a situation involving myself and an old friend, I just kept remembering all of the negative things about our friendship. When I invoked the energy of Jeremiel, a quiet voice in my head said, 'It's time to send love,' and it gave me the inspiration I needed to change my thoughts. Jeremiel always helps us to remember that love is the answer.

Invoking Jeremiel

Archangel Jeremiel can help you to become a miracle-worker. In my eyes, a miracle-worker is someone who changes the basis of their thoughts and actions from fear to love and acceptance.

Jeremiel also helps you to accept your spiritual innocence. Even though there may be things you wish you could go back and change or heal, the only way forwards is to accept your wholeness and recognize that same wholeness in others. (In the next chapter, we take this remembering to a deeper level.)

✧   You can invoke Archangel Jeremiel through many different modalities, but the great thing about this book is the fact that he's on the cover. You can use this as a meditation tool to welcome him.

✧   Alternatively, keeping your eyes open, follow these words:

'I am safe, well and protected.

A golden light of heaven washes over my whole being.

At this time I open up my heart and welcome in the blessings of Archangel Jeremiel.

Jeremiel the archangel stands before me with his torch of illumination.

As Jeremiel moves into my energy, I surrender any resistance. I open up and welcome in his light.'

✧ Or you might like to try this prayer:

> 'Thank you, Archangel Jeremiel, for drawing close and for revealing yourself to me in ways I can understand, whether they be physical signs or subtle reminders. I now welcome your guidance and support as I allow myself to fully accept and understand forgiveness. With your help I know I can perceive forgiveness as it is and I know I can offer this gift to myself and to others on a daily basis.
>
> I now leave behind all past resistance and fear, I surrender what I no longer need and I crack open the walls that surround my heart so that I can reveal my inner truth. There is a pure light shining inside me and I know, Jeremiel, that you can see it. Thank you for seeing my spiritual truth and thank you for removing the illusions from my vision so I can see it, too. Thank you for showing me how to forgive and who to forgive and thank you for helping me see that I am forgiven.
>
> I accept my spiritual innocence and from this point onwards I will remember that forgiveness is a natural part of my spiritual identity. I walk now through the doors of freedom, with you at my side, a friend and leader.
>
> I forgive and I am forgiven.
>
> And so it is!'

✧ After the invocation or the prayer, see the light of Jeremiel washing over you, your life and anyone you feel needs it. See it extending to your past, present and future.

The invocation is complete.

Chapter 4
THE UNREALITY OF SIN

'This is the way salvation works. As you step back, the light in you steps forward and encompasses the world.'
A Course in Miracles, Lesson 156

Now you know that you have Mary Magdalene with you as the guide and demonstration of forgiveness, Archangel Jeremiel to help you on the path to forgiveness and your forgiveness angel who is dedicated to you unleashing miracles in your life, it's time to move ahead on this journey.

One of the fundamental challenges with forgiveness, especially self-forgiveness, is releasing guilt. The voice of guilt is a challenging one and we've all heard it. Whenever we've made a mistake or done something that we later wish we hadn't, this overpowering voice comes in and makes us cringe. It makes us feel uptight and embarrassed to be ourselves. It makes us feel alone.

Vulnerability

In order to help you with guilt, I suppose it's important to come clean about my own life and put myself in the vulnerable space that many of you will find yourselves in. As far as I'm concerned, vulnerability is cool. It's good to expose the real you, because then you're so much closer to loving yourself than when you're pretending that you're safe while hiding behind something.

So, I have to say I've heard the voice of guilt when I've said something that's been out of place or hurtful to others and also when I haven't done something I feel I should have done, like my yoga practice. Sometimes even the silliest of situations will come into my mind and make me feel awkward and guilty.

One of my major challenges in life has been my relationship with food and my body. When I was younger, I spent time in a wheelchair and in a children's hospital because I had a virus that left me paralyzed. I remember that I didn't enjoy food during that time, and I especially didn't enjoy hospital food. As I got better, though, so did my relationship with food, and I became a fit and healthy kid.

When my parents divorced, I moved from Port Glasgow to Greenock and changed schools. It only took me a few days to make friends at my new school and it wasn't too bad. The truth is, though, that I never really enjoyed school and inwardly my little old self would always be saying, 'Why am I even learning this?' or 'I don't want to be here.'

I never felt that I fitted in entirely. I was a complete dreamer and would spend afternoons staring into space, much to the teachers' dismay. As I grew, my sensitivity became so strong that if someone teased me or played a prank on me I'd take it to heart. I'd get so upset by the comments and teasing of my friends.

When I felt down or overly sensitive I didn't know how to get rid of the feeling – until, around the age of 10, I realized that if I ate too much, I wouldn't feel as much. If I ate and ate, the teasing words of the other kids, or even the forcefulness of the teachers, wouldn't matter any longer.

This created a huge spiral in my life and very quickly I went from long-legged, skinny little Kyle to a chubby kid who really resented his whole body.

When I found spirituality, I decided that becoming vegetarian was important for my growth because I didn't want to feel guilty over eating animals or consuming the dead bodies of other beings. That was fine, but my relationship with food was still not good. I was vegetarian, but I wasn't healthy in the slightest. I didn't consume meat, but I still ate heaps of heavy, deep-fried, high-fat and high-carb foods, and before I knew it I was what a doctor would call clinically obese. In fact, I went up and down in weight like a yo-yo and I tried every single trick in the book – diets, teas, CD programmes, personal nutritionists and more. And this went on for years! Every time I made a change for the better, I'd fall back off the wagon and eat even more than I had in the first place. I'd feel guilty for overeating and then I'd feel guilty for feeling overweight. When I felt guilty, I'd eat, and when I felt fat, I'd eat even more – it was a really vicious circle to be in.

Even though I had this going on, the angels still worked with and through me – they didn't see me in the monstrous light in which I saw myself, and I knew they loved me even though I found it really difficult to love myself.

I remember when my first book was published seeing myself in newspapers, on TV and in photographs and realizing that my body wasn't reflecting my teaching. I was telling people that they needed to love and forgive themselves, and even though I knew this was true, a part of me felt like a phoney because I didn't entirely love myself either.

My mum saved the day again! She started a new healthy-living plan because she, too, had got to a point where she just wasn't happy in her body. She told me that after being at my first 'I Can Do It' conference with me she'd decided she needed to physically reflect the love that we'd been telling everyone about, so she'd decided to join Slimming World.

When my mum joined the club, truth be told I was sceptical. I thought that it wouldn't work for me. 'Come on, just give it a chance,' she said. 'It's great – you can eat loads on it and it's normal food!' I chose not to believe her.

After her first week at the club, she lost 3lbs and came home completely buzzing about her achievement. She tried to encourage me to join again and said that I'd really love it.

I replied, 'If the angels can give me some sort of sign that it's the right choice for me, then I'll do it.'

I remember going into my bedroom and saying to the angels mentally, 'Thank you, angels, for sending a sign to show me if this is the right weight-loss plan for me.'

That weekend it was Glasgow's International Angel Day, an event that I run annually with my friend Diane. We sponsor a local children's charity and it's always really well received.

We had over 200 people coming to join us that day. Mum was on the door and getting people to their seats as I was organizing the charity raffle tickets for those coming in. Just as I was about to open the afternoon programme, I saw her wave me over.

When I went to speak to her, she said, 'See that lady in the front row there, with the black hair and the red blouse?'

'Yes,' I said, wondering what she was going to say.

'That's the lady who runs my Slimming World class. I didn't know she was interested in angels!'

Did the sign need to be any clearer? That day at the angel event I decided to surrender to the journey of loving my body and accepting myself.

A week later I went with my mum to the Slimming World class and got weighed in. I was much heavier than I'd expected, but I decided to follow the journey, and being there with my mum was a huge motivation to us both. We bought heart-shaped plates, new cutlery and began to follow the plan. (I did the vegetarian version.) And week by week, the weight began to leave my body.

I remember asking the angels, 'What more would support my growth to weight loss?'

They told me, 'Feel safe and practise yoga.'

It made so much sense. I knew I needed to feel safe. My body had created a huge shield of a belly around me because I didn't really want to be seen and I didn't want anyone to hack into my sensitivity. I wasn't quite sure how to go about feeling safe, but I knew I could practise yoga. I'd been going every week to a class, so now I started going four to five times a week.

Within a space of a few months, around 30lbs had come off and I decided to take yoga to the next level, so I signed up for yoga teacher-training. Actually, I accidentally signed up for Ashtanga yoga teacher-training – and I didn't have a clue about that.

The first day of yoga teacher-training, the first thing I noticed was that I was the biggest in the class in body size. The second thing that came to my attention was that I was the only boy there apart from the teacher.

The training started at 6 a.m. with a practice for the teacher to 'assess how deep into our practice' we were. I was in for a shock. He spoke in Sanskrit and he was tough. What I thought was a workout was a warm-up to him, and what I thought was yoga, wasn't. My classmates were doing serious moves, standing on their hands and their head and, for me, the voice of fear, guilt, fatness and unfitness was kicking right in. I felt like crying.

All day long, feelings of not fitting in came rushing back to me, and it was scary to say the least. I went back to my hotel sore, both emotionally and physically, wondering why I'd signed up in the first place. And why had I chosen this style of yoga?! Ashtanga is one of the most physical forms of yoga there is. It demands not only flexibility but also body and core strength. What had I been thinking?

I began to sob. All I wanted was to feel safe in my body and there I was in a hotel on a course for which I didn't even fit the criteria...

Change

After lying on the couch for a while, wondering what to do, I called my mum (as usual), and she told me to 'stick in there' and that it would be 'worth it in the end'. She was right, of course. But I didn't have the strength, I couldn't do half of the moves and though I'd thought I was flexible, when it came to this course I was as stiff as a board.

I went home, hit the floor in cross-legged meditation position and called out to my angels. Why did I feel so guilty about my body – its shape, size and flexibility? I wanted to change, but at the same time I was so scared of it that it seemed easier to give up.

A simple message poured into my mind: 'Love yourself enough to change!'

That's what I needed to hear! It came into my mind that feeling guilty and frustrated wasn't helping me to change. I needed to move into loving myself and loving the whole situation. I needed to shift my reality to encompass forgiveness and I needed to do it with an open heart. I didn't want to blame anyone or anything for how I felt about my body – my relationship with food was what it was because that was all I'd known at the time, but now I was on the road to recovery.

I remembered the quote from *A Course in Miracles*: 'Forgiveness is an earthly form of love' (Lesson 186).

I was ready to work on my full-body forgiveness and I was ready to love myself enough to change. It wasn't about where I'd come from and it wasn't about where I was going. I was ready to forgive myself here and now and I was going to do that in a loving way.

So I stuck to my healthy-living vegetarian food and added to my daily spiritual practice yoga and affirmations that made me feel loving about my body. I'd practise the Ashtanga Primary Sequence to the best of my ability and when I was lying on my mat afterwards I'd place my hands on my belly and say things like:

'There is no place safer than in my body!'

'I love and forgive myself.'

'I forgive and I am forgiven.'

'My body now returns to its natural state of health.'

'It feels so good to be healthy and happy! I am well!'

Over the following months the transformation was outstanding: I lost another 30lbs, bringing me up to a total loss of 65lbs at that point, and I felt absolutely great.

That might sound like the end of the story, but now and then I can still hear the voice of inner doubt, the voice that likes to tell me that I should feel ashamed, fat and aware of the stretch marks I have on my body, but I choose to reply in a loving way!

Anytime I hear the negative remarks of my ego, I tell myself, 'You are safe here and you are loved by angels beyond words!'

Guilt

Guilt is a challenging aspect of self-love and forgiveness, and we've all felt it. I know for a fact that you've felt guilty in your life and you may not even know why.

I've found that guilt may seem natural but, as we saw earlier, the truth is that the natural way of being is love. Anything that comes from fear is a complete illusion, and guilt is the cousin of fear. To me, it's the ego's challenge to forgiveness. It's the voice that's saying, 'But are you *sure* you want to step into love? Are you *sure* you want freedom?' As hard as it may seem at times, the answer is most definitely: 'Yes!'

As far as I'm concerned, guilt has a lot to do with the way we were brought up. I'm not passing the blame to my parents and teachers or yours – it's just the way that people have coped with the information they've had. The ego has led us to believe that we need to be in control, so we judge what's going on around us and try to change it. We don't realize that if we step out of the way, love takes control.

For example, when I was growing up, everywhere I'd go I'd be told I was a good boy or a bad boy. Well, to be honest I don't remember my parents telling me I was 'bad' ever, but when I was at school, if I did something 'wrong', I'd be told that I was a 'bad boy' and that began to create thoughts of guilt inside me. All the way through school I was never publicly praised when I was good, but I was pointed out when I was bad, and if I'm honest it probably made me do more things 'wrong' so I'd get more attention.

Most of us rate our self-worth, too, on 'good' and 'bad' – on how well we're doing or how well we've done. This is also something we learn growing up. Winning a race at school makes you instantly cooler than the others, and I never won any races, so I always felt that I wasn't as good as those around me. And in the classroom, if your marks aren't as good as those of your classmates, you don't make it to university… and you don't get the job, the relationship, the car, and so on. That same mentality followed me, as it follows most of us, on into adulthood. What if we could see it differently?

Could you imagine what it would be like if you were just told you were good? Imagine being told you were good from the moment you were born all the way through your childhood, including all through the education system, by every parent, guardian, teacher, leader and more… Your life would be so different and you'd feel a lot less guilty.

Types of Guilt

I've realized that there are different types of guilt. Here's what I've found.

Performance

A great deal of guilt comes from how well we've done – or haven't done. It kicks in when we haven't got a certain amount of money in the bank, gained a particular qualification or, even worse, got very many Twitter followers.

Performance or achievement-based guilt is so common, especially if someone has already set a standard that they're expecting us to reach or we already have certain expectations of ourselves.

Comparison

Guilt can also come from comparing ourselves to someone else. We learn it in childhood – it's particularly common with siblings – and then move through life comparing ourselves with other people. We'll find ourselves saying, 'Oh, you're so much better than me at that,' or even, 'You've done better than I have,' and then we'll feel guilty for not being the same as our neighbour. But as soon as we compare ourselves to someone else we forget about our individual light that's shining so brightly!

Judgement

What happens when we look in the mirror and don't see what we want? We may have marks or scars or be a shape that doesn't make us happy. We may judge ourselves as not looking good enough. And then we'll feel guilty for not being what society expects of us or, even worse, what someone else expects of us. But when we have guilt based on judgement, we've failed to see the divinity that the angels see in us every given second.

Shame

Many people are faced with guilt because they're ashamed of who they are. I've encountered people in this day and age who have felt deep shame because of the colour of their skin, the area or country they were brought up in or even their sexuality. Shame is a challenging place to be, but the truth is that in the eyes of your angel you are perfect no matter who you are. You are a great light to them.

Sin

Many people feel guilty because they think they're disappointing God. This is one of the most challenging forms of guilt for me to help people with, because there are so many people out there throwing this down our throats. The truth is that God is love and therefore not holding anything against us because in love there is no judgement and there are no grievances. As we saw previously in 'The Gospel of Mary Magdalene', Jesus said, 'There is no sin.'

In my eyes, sin is forgetting that love exists. The literal interpretation of the word is that something has gone contrary to plan, and what I've learned is that God's plan for us is love and it's a 'sin' when we forget it. The truth is we can never disappoint God because we are an extension of His love.

Realizing Our Infinite Worth

I run a monthly spiritual group called the Angel Club in Renfrew. People come from all over Scotland and we spend our evening focusing on angels. We regularly bring in guest speakers and I also share my thoughts on a spiritual subject and give angel readings.

I recently held an open coaching session at the club, in which I spoke about the power of forgiveness. It was a really heartwarming evening, as a lot of people joined me in sharing their vulnerability with the rest of the group. One lady, Linda, put up her hand as we were speaking about forgiveness and told me that she felt guilty but there was no apparent reason for her to feel it.

She told us that she'd been brought up in a home where she'd just been made to feel bad. Her mother hadn't been the most loving of parents; in fact, she'd regretted ever having children and had made it obvious. So Linda had grown up in a place where she wasn't wanted and had gone through the 60 years of her life feeling guilty for being alive. She opened up to the group with tears pouring from her eyes, desperate to release the pain.

I was completely blown away by her vulnerability. Here she was, standing in front of us and sharing her challenge in complete confidence. The truth was, I didn't know how it could be healed, so I closed my eyes, took a deep breath and then, as I exhaled, said inwardly, 'Thank you, angels, for revealing the cure to this guilt!'

I then heard a simple and profound reply: 'You can heal guilt by realizing your own infinite worth. You are enough!'

Guilt, as I mentioned earlier, is the cousin of fear, and when the ego voice pumps it into our mind, we can allow it to run the show – or not. We can choose either fear or love, and when we allow love to come to the forefront of our mind, we shift our perception and so create a miracle. We also crack our heart open and can then give and receive the love that we deserve – and that includes self-love.

We are enough – that is to say, *good* enough – and the angels want us to realize that. They love us unconditionally and they know that we've done our best up to this point. These holy messengers of God also want us to know that their Creator loves us dearly and if we can realize how beautifully perfect we are in His eyes, we'll begin to feel that love.

Sure, the voice of guilt will pop up now and then, but every time it does we can just say this simple affirmation: 'I am enough!' or, even better: 'In the eyes of God I am unconditional love!' and bit by bit we'll clear the way.

Our mind is like a garden – it likes to be tended. Every time we tackle fear-based thoughts, we're taking out the weeds, and every time we remind ourselves that we are love, we plant a beautiful rosebush in their place.

Hearing this message was important for Linda and the rest of the group that evening and to bring our meeting to a close we did a meditation accepting that we were enough.

I remember seeing tears and hearing cries of relief from all those there that night as they released what they no longer needed and accepted that they were really enough.

Accepting that we are enough reminds me once again of the passage from 'The Gospel of Mary Magdalene' when Jesus said: 'That is why Good came into your midst, coming to the good that belongs to every nature, in order to restore it to its root.'

Releasing guilt is coming back into the good that belongs to us! Forgiving ourselves is loving ourselves enough to realize that we are the Good and the Good belongs to us.

Surrender

Mary Magdalene, Jesus and the angels are waiting by you now and they're there to help you to release the guilt that's not serving your divine purpose, which is to be happy.

Whenever your voice of guilt gets too loud, the most important things to know are:

✧ In God's eyes you are good enough.

✧ You are an expression of love.

✧ The Earth is blessed to have you here.

✧ Angels gather around you.

✧ You are loving and lovable.

✧ You are deserving of peace simply because you *are*.

The next phase of moving into change is loving yourself enough to realize that you deserve to forgive yourself for feeling guilty in the first place. Allow the angels to remove your guilt through this affirmative prayer:

> 'Thank you, angels, for standing around me now as I reveal my true self.
>
> I am a divine spark of unconditional love and I accept my wholeness and holiness now.
>
> I surrender now into your arms the ideas of guilt, shame and sin. With this surrender, I release them from my vision.
>
> I am filled with light as I remember that I am good and I deserve only good.
>
> It feels so good knowing that I don't walk this journey alone – that I am held by you and guided by your wings.
>
> I am enough and I am unconditional love accepted by God and his angels!
>
> And so it is!'

Chapter 5
HEALING THE CLOUD OF GRIEF

*'Be not forgetful to entertain strangers, for thereby
some have entertained angels unawares.'*
HEBREWS, CHAPTER 13, VERSE 2

I was sleeping but I was awake. I'd been out in the city with my friends earlier and we'd been dancing and laughing. After one beer on the dance floor, though, I'd decided that I'd just take it easy for the rest of the night and enjoy the company. It had been so good to be home, as I'd just been in various spots all over Europe sharing my message about angels. It had been quite late when I'd got home, so I'd gone straight to bed and fallen into a deep sleep. Now, about seven hours later, I was having the most vivid dream – it was like a clairvoyant vision.

In the dream, I realized I was dreaming. I learned only last year, from my friend Charlie Morley, that dreams like this are called lucid dreams and we can interact with them if we choose. What I decided to do was surrender all sense of control and know the divine was present with me.

I found myself hovering above a great stone. I could see a pair of hands using stonemason's tools to carve into it. They were carving the symbol that is known as the *vesica piscis*.

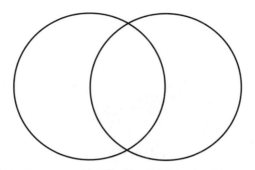

The *vesica piscis*

I knew this symbol was important and I knew it had connections to Mary Magdalene, but I remember thinking, *Why is this here in my dream?*

Then suddenly I saw a cave. In front of it was a vision of Mary Magdalene. She was draped in a red veil and her robes were deep purple, like aubergine. She was starting to move towards me.

On either side of her was an angel, but these were totally unlike any angels I'd ever seen before. First off, they were identical. They were neither male nor female, but beings of pure light. Their faces looked like the sun shining and their eyes seemed very deep. They wore robes that were made of a silky material I'd never seen before and they were swirling around their bodies. They did have wings, but those wings were made of pure light.

Standing completely still, heart pounding, jaw dropping in complete amazement, I could feel tears of joy pouring from my eyes. The two angels were drawing closer to me now while Mary Magdalene stopped and looked on as if she knew what was happening.

I could feel intense heat moving over my body as the angels approached. If my heart was to be a door, it was wide open. Every hair of my body was standing on end with what I call 'angel bumps', but I didn't feel scared because I could sense love. I was just full of anticipation because I didn't know what was going to happen next.

I decided that since I was awake in my dream and I was allowed to have some input, I needed to ask the angels why they were there. So, gaining courage and momentum, I said, 'Who are you and what would you like to share?'

The haunting words of the beings began to flow into my mind:

'We are the Myriam, hear our call.

We come to you in a state of grace.

We represent unified love and are the angels who came to Mary of Magdala as told in the gospels.

With our light we can help you awaken a state of grace within.

It is time to leave behind all grief and fears of separation, for the light of source is forever within.

This light is known as Christ.

It is the Holy Spirit and it is present within you now.

Welcome us and allow us to awaken your holy vision so you can perceive the light of Christ within you and all of humanity.'

With that, the angels and Mary became one, just like the *vesica piscis* symbol, and vanished.

I instantly woke up.

I sat up in bed and rubbed my eyes, wondering if it was just a dream. Then I jumped out of bed and ran to see my mum.

She looked at me, saying, 'What was in the house there?'

I replied, 'You're not going to believe what just happened to me!'

As I began to tell my mum the story, I realized that something profound had just gone down. The Myriam had mentioned that they were the angels who had visited Mary Magdalene 'as told in the gospels' and it occurred to me that they were her guardian angels and that they were still working with her from the other side. Together they were a team, as revealed by the *vesica piscis*. The two circles of this symbol represented the angels coming together and the central oval shape represented Mary herself. Three individual energies combined to create one. It was magnificent.

I had doubts, though, about whether I should reveal this vision to others. I mean, who was I to say I'd encountered biblical angels and the beautiful ascended teacher who was the beloved devotee of Jesus? I meditated for days on it, but I knew that I had to trust what I'd heard. It had meaning and it would help others.

Thinking about the Myriam, I realized I needed to find out more about them, their message and the gifts they offered to Earth. Were these beings like other angels? Could they be called on by anyone?

The first thing I wanted to know more about was their name. Myriam – what did it mean? I found that Miriam was another name for Mary, which made sense. But the angels had ensured I knew in some way that their name was spelled with a 'y', not an 'i'.

After some looking around online, I found that *Myr* was an Egyptian word for 'love' or 'beloved' – and then I had the lightbulb moment. If *Myr* means 'beloved' and we keep 'iam' as it is, the message in the angels' name is: 'The beloved I am.' When I saw that, every single hair on my body stood on end. Mary Magdalene has been known as 'the beloved' for hundreds of years.

The next part of my initiation with the Myriam was discovering their gifts. I thought back to the story told in the Gospel of John. Mary had been on her knees, grieving not only over the loss of Jesus's life but also his physical body. It had been while she was sobbing at his tomb that the two angels had appeared and had asked her why she was crying.

I realized that the Myriam angels had *healed* the grief within Mary – these divine angelic beings of pure white light had absorbed that deepest, most tragic of emotions. Not only that, they had awakened her clairvoyant vision: it was after seeing them that she encountered the risen Christ.

Just like everyone, Mary was human – she had emotions and she was deeply saddened to be separated from her teacher. The angels helped remove that feeling of separateness so that she could perceive the healed Jesus and could continue her mission to awaken 'the Good' in others.

It reminded me that angels can indeed come to us when we are in despair. They can save us from our worst nightmare. They can even intervene to get us out of a situation – like a car crash or a burning building – if it's not our time to go or if going through that experience is going to block our spiritual purpose.

Even if our mind isn't able to accept the help, through the divine spiritual laws angels can override our unwillingness, particularly if our soul requires an adjustment to get us back on our path. They can heal us through grace.

It's clear that Mary Magdalene's spiritual purpose was to share the wonderful news of goodness with the world and if she hadn't been healed of her grief, she wouldn't have been able to see Jesus for who he was or get past the challenge of his crucifixion. When the angels came to her, they helped her to reach a state of ultimate calm in which all resistance to spirit was removed so she could have the holy encounter with Jesus. That would become one of her most significant life events and lead to her becoming the teacher she is today and her lessons being passed on through her gospel.

Awakening Our Holy Vision

In order for us to move through forgiveness, grief has to be lifted from our heart, too. Grief is something we all know. It's that emotion that comes over us when we feel alone and forgotten. It's the heart-wrenching fear that tries to convince us that we're never going to be the same again. Fortunately, it's a complete illusion and the truth rests silently within us and is just waiting to welcome us back. Angels are ready to guide us there.

When grief is lifted, forgiveness becomes easier because then we can see light for what it is, and that's when we see spirit. To do this, we need to forget the feeling of separateness that haunts us all and remember love. The angels that surround us are a constant source and reminder of love. They whisper gently into our soul and they encourage us to listen. They want us to know that we're never separate from those we love. In some deep inner silence, we are connected to everyone and everything that ever has been and ever will be. We are everything. We are love.

It's when we remember love that we're reminded of it even more. That's why people who believe in angels experience them more or receive reminders of heaven: because they've chosen to remember that it's there.

The holy vision that the Myriam angels offer us is the removal of the blindfold. They are here to shake us from our worst nightmare and bring us home. These divine guardian angels of Mary Magdalene help us to heal so we can perceive holiness in all.

Call for Healing

The story of Mary Magdalene seeing Jesus completely healed is a powerful allegorical story, because it refers to something we'll all encounter in one way or another. We'll all feel separate from what we love at some point in our life and it will take deep dedication to remember that we're not separate at all. The great thing is that there is help.

If you're ready to heal any grief or grievances in your life it means you're ready to move past the fear that what you love can be taken from you. When you're ready to heal from this nightmare emotion, you move into the realization that you are one with what you love – you are one with all. You also remember that within the silence of your heart awaits the connection to home, to all those who have departed from this Earth and to those who feel distant through time and space, and it is then that you perceive your holy spirit, or what the Myriam call 'Christ'.

The Myriam help us to look beyond grief, guilt and fear. They help us to awaken the vision of grace and remember that we are never separate from God, for the light of Christ is within us all. When I say 'Christ', I'm not talking about Jesus Christ, but the inner consciousness that is holy and always will be – the real you, which you may even call 'Buddha' or 'consciousness'.

So, you can call on the Myriam to:

✧ help you deal with the loss of a loved one

✧ heal from any guilt or fear that's left after a passing

✧ overcome any deep-rooted emotions connected to feeling separate from God, angels or spirit

✧ awaken the vision of grace (so you can perceive light in others, too)

✧ honour your inner divinity

Call to the Myriam:

> *'Divine Holy Angels of Mary Magdalene, pure white beings known as the Myriam, I call on you now.*
>
> *I am ready and willing to remember the silence of love that waits within the cave of my heart. Thank you for awakening within me the state of grace in which you bless others and for helping me see to life through the eyes of love.*
>
> *At this time I step into my spiritual power and recharge the senses that help me to see. Let my eyes see the light in all of humanity.*
>
> *I recognize that on a physical level I may not experience the connectedness that sleeps within me and choose now to go beyond the limitations of my body and of the Earth so that I can clearly see the love at a deeper level.*
>
> *As I embrace the gifts that I have come to this world with, my body begins to accept them and I begin to embody the truth and light that I am.*
>
> *I am never separate from those I love – I am forever with them in mind, body and soul. I am love.*
>
> *May this initiation be completed as I surrender to your capable light.*
>
> *And so it is!'*

Chapter 6
REMEMBERING ONLY LOVING THOUGHTS

'Divine things must be loved to be known.'
Blaise Pascal, French scientist and philosopher

'Forgiveness is remembering only loving thoughts,' according to *A Course in Miracles*, and it's true. When it comes to practising forgiveness and returning to the inner peace that is constantly offered to us, there has to be a choice. We always have a choice – we can choose love or choose fear. When we're faced with a challenging situation or something comes in our direction that feels painful, instantly the ego voice will begin to throw up a range of defences and we'll feel as if there's pressure to choose one of them. But while all of that's going on, within us there is a certain silence and within that silence there is love. When we decide to move into that space, the only solution that the voice of our soul will present us with will be complete acceptance.

When something is hurtful, sure we feel it, but it doesn't have to be *real*. As we learned earlier, *A Course in Miracles* calls anything that isn't love an illusion and I really resonate with this way of thinking. Even though we've all experienced pain in the past and will experience it in the future, the truth is that deep within the pit of our soul, peace and light are just desperate to shine though.

At moments of pain, the ego is doing its job too, because it's telling us that we're being attacked. In fact, it's probably doing a little more than that – it's telling us to defend ourselves with an explanation or an earthly experience that determines our worth. We don't have to fall into the trap, though. When we're faced with fear, we can choose to lean back into the wings of forgiveness.

That may not be all there is to it, of course. One thing I know I've found difficult on the journey of forgiveness is when someone goes out their way to be mean, hurtful or threatening. I can move into forgiveness, sure, but another part of me always wants to know the reason *why* someone feels it's OK to attack me or someone else. Every now and then someone will throw a spanner in the works and question me and my services, for instance. They'll choose to create an opinion, but really they don't know where I'm coming from, the work I've done up to this point or how I'm serving others.

I remember two years ago I kept seeing a robin redbreast in my meditations. I loved seeing the little robin. They're fierce little birds. I remember during one meditation I got an insight about them. I decided to share it on my Facebook page, which had around 4,000 followers at the time. I found a photograph of a robin and put the information I'd received on it: 'When a robin redbreast constantly visits you or crosses your path, a loved one in heaven is trying to say, "Hello! I'm with you!"'

The picture got so much attention, it was crazy! In fact, within a few weeks it had racked up over 25,000 Facebook shares. That means over 50,000 people had seen my post. This was cool because I wanted people to have an uplifting message and to share what I'd received from the angels.

At the same time, however, there was an influx of challenging people on my page, attacking my work and how much I charged for private sessions and saying that I was a complete scam artist. I remember reading some of the comments. They were just degrading. One man wrote on my wall that I didn't deserve to be alive and should go and kill myself! I remember feeling sick and shaking all over. Here was I, doing my bit to help the world to be a brighter place and at the same time being chastised for it. I just didn't know what to do.

I had a long think about it. There was no way I was allowing myself to be a victim – I needed to change my energy. When I was being attacked, I needed to affirm and really know in my heart that my soul was completely whole. I knew that when I remembered who I really was, I'd be protected.

Know Help Is Here

Angels have taught me that yes, we can ask for help and we can ask for protection, but when we really *know* that we are being held and protected and that we are completely safe, the whole dynamics of our energy change. It reminds me of this wonderful quote from Lesson 183 of *A Course in Miracles*:

> *'God's Name cannot be heard without response, nor said without an echo in the mind that calls you to remember. Say His Name, and you invite the angels to surround the ground on which you stand, and sing to you as they spread out their wings to keep you safe, and shelter you from every worldly thought that would intrude upon your holiness.'*

Nothing can take our holiness away, but the truth is that certain people and situations can encourage us to forget it. It is in these circumstances that we need to return to miraculous thinking by remembering only loving thoughts. It is our only refuge.

What is miraculous thinking? It's that shift of perception from fear to love. So, whenever someone has thrown something upsetting in our direction, we can send love right back. The truth is when someone begins to scourge us with their words or actions, they've forgotten about love. Most importantly, they've forgotten about loving themselves. We can share our love with them by sending them positive thoughts.

A Course in Miracles says, '…If you want peace, you must give up the idea of conflict entirely and for all time,' and it's true. If you want to get the idea of being attacked out of your life, you need to get the idea out of your mind. When a mind has let go of conflict and only recognizes a willingness to create peace, peace is inevitable.

So, when I was slated online by hundreds of people, my mum and I worked tirelessly deleting and blocking every negative comment or act of fear from my page. I wanted to keep reflecting loving thoughts so that people would be reminded of the angels, so I kept posting my daily updates on love, prayer and angels. And whenever anyone said anything to upset me or divert me from my holiness, I sent them love. I believe that when we send love to someone, their angels kiss their forehead and massage the tension out of their head. They whisper sweet loving reminders in their ear and pray tirelessly that they remember the love that waits within. So I took note of each disruptive person's name and visualized them being held by angels, being kissed on the forehead by archangels and being wrapped in a pink blanket of love – and then I let it go!

It's not nice when you feel attacked or held up by someone else's challenges – especially when you feel you're doing good work. The truth is, I could have begun to list the charities I donate to monthly, the places where I volunteer and the number of times I give free sessions to those in need, but what would it have proved? That someone wanted me to prove my light and my holiness through material actions, when the truth was my holiness wasn't something that could be seen, it was something that was felt by the heart. So I shared it in a way I knew worked: I sent love.

When we come under attack or a situation begins to haunt us, we must find a way of realigning ourselves with what we know to be true. We have to realign our thoughts with God (love), so that we can move on feeling supported rather than separate from our source. What I've found from personal experience is that as soon as I move into fear, I lose my sense of connection to God and move into a place where I feel victimized and alone. The truth is, of course, that angels are standing by me, desperate to help me.

There's a quote by the 19th-century Italian priest and writer St John Bosco that I think helps us to understand the nature of our angels versus our ego self. He says:

> *'When tempted, invoke your angel. He is more eager to help you than you are to be helped! Ignore the devil, and do not be afraid of him. He trembles and flees at your guardian angel's sight.'*

Most of the time our guardian angel is just waiting for our invitation to help. Angels are always more eager to help us than we are to be helped. When we shift our focus to receiving the support that we deserve, they will come in and change the energy surrounding us and the challenges facing us. In this case, the devil is not some crazy demon but more the negative voice or the memory of something that has challenged us.

In truth, I don't believe in a devil, because I don't believe in a hell. I believe the devil is the ego voice, the inner doubt system within, and I believe hell is when we allow the ego to run the show instead of our divine guidance system.

Angels to the Rescue

Angels have the ability to support us when we're in despair. They can override our free will and help us even if we don't ask, if what's happening isn't part of our karma or assigned lessons. This is why you'll hear stories of people being saved by an unseen presence or having a visit from an angel when they're in a deep depression – the angels were sent by God to save them. I've found that even though angels can do this, they still find it much easier if we align ourselves with love. When we say an affirmative prayer, combine it with gratitude, visualize ourselves surrounded by a golden light and meditate, we raise our vibration to that of the angels. To put it simply, angels are divine light and when we visualize ourselves surrounded by light, we become magnets for the support of these tremendous beings.

If we have negative thoughts based on a grievance or a feeling of being attacked, then we must know that attack isn't real – it's an illusion. A person can say things to us and even physically hurt our body, but our true self can never be hurt – our soul is eternal. And when we begin to align our thoughts, mediation practice and prayers to love, angels will wrap their wings of protection and forgiveness around us.

When someone is threatening us or is hurting us physically or emotionally, they're harming themselves, too. Lesson 26 of A Course in Miracles talks of attack thoughts. In my terms, it tells us that when we think about someone in a negative way or want to attack them with insults or by pointing out their weaknesses, we believe that we, too, can be attacked. That's one vicious circle! The affirmation on this reads:

My attack thoughts are attacking my invulnerability.

This is so true. In God's eyes we're invulnerable, but *our* thoughts create *our* reality – not God's. So, what the *Course* is teaching is when we attack another person, we're inevitably attacking ourselves!

Here's the idea set out clearly in the lesson:

The idea for today introduces the thought that you always attack yourself first. If attack thoughts must entail the belief that you are vulnerable, their effect is to weaken you in your own eyes. Thus they have attacked your perception of yourself. And because you believe in them, you can no longer believe in yourself. A false image of yourself has come to take the place of what you are.

When we move into judgement, forgiveness can't take place, and when we're busy with attack thoughts, we're leaving ourselves wide open to be attacked, too. In the context of forgiveness, there's only one way out of this state, and that's by creating a diversion to love.

A Diversion to Love

✧   If you're ever about to judge someone and launch into attack thoughts, try saying this:

'At this moment I surrender all negative and attack thoughts to God.

I remember that I am united with God.

Within my heart shines the light of my Creator.

When I remember His name, an echo of love moves through my life.

When I call on His name, angels of light surround my being.

Love is who I am and I take this moment to remember.

All illusions are released when I focus on love.

I return to the natural state of who I am.

I am love.'

✧ As you say this, visualize light surrounding you and radiating from your heart.

✧ Imagine the light moving to the situation or person that you're working on forgiving. That can be you, too!

✧ See in your mind angelic beings swirling around you, keeping you safe and honouring the fact that as you release your attack thoughts, you return to safety.

Sending Angels of Love and Harmony

Sending love isn't difficult at all. It's all about intention. You can just think of someone, feel love deep in your heart, intend it to reach them and you've done the job. I always use prayer and visualization, however, because it's a powerful combination. And there are two archangels I call on in particular when I want to create harmony and send love to a person or a situation. They're always so willing to help.

The first of the two is Archangel Raguel, whose name means 'Friend of God'. He's a handsome angel who has a soft and feminine face – in fact, for years I was unsure whether he was presenting as male or female. He always shows up in my mind's eye with piercing blue eyes, short, sun-kissed hair and a sparkling orangey-gold aura. He is one of the angels of justice and his main spiritual purpose is to bring harmony. He wants us all to be in harmony, and that includes those who are challenging us. He's absolutely loving and consistent in his support to all those who call on him and his priority is that everyone finds peace.

The other archangel is Chamuel. In looks, this powerful archangel always reminds me of David Bowie in the 80s. He has an amazingly bright ruby robe and his almost white hair can disappear into his graceful white aura. His name means 'He who sees God' and even just looking at the meaning of that, you can see exactly what he's all about: he's the angel who sees God, and to me, God is exactly the same as love, so he's the angel who sees love. His soul purpose is to help us to remember love. He can help us to find the divine in our worst enemy, he can help us to discover love in a challenge and most importantly he can help us see love in ourselves. His presence alone expands our heart centre.

These two angels are a powerful combination of harmony and love, and they are here now, standing by to bring a sense of balance to your life. Whether you're working on forgiveness for yourself or someone else or a particular issue, these angels can help you to grasp the possibility of change and help you send and accept love. Call on them now, or anytime you need them, and allow them to support you.

Here are some prayers to help you:

A Prayer to Welcome Love and Harmony

Powerful archangels who look upon me as a friend, thank you for sending your peaceful warrior angels Chamuel and Raguel in my direction. It feels so good to know that I am being surrounded by a light of peace.

Thank you, Chamuel, for unlocking within me the vision of love and awakening acceptance in the space of my heart. I welcome your loving presence and I am grateful that you can help me to see the good within myself and others.

Thank you, Raguel, for pouring a wave of harmonious energy over my entire being. I allow my cells to be nurtured and my mind to be calmed by your presence. I know that from this point there is always a fair and positive way forwards.

I am held by love and harmony is my only solution!

And so it is!

A Prayer to Send Love and Harmony

Thank you, Archangel Chamuel and Archangel Raguel, for blessing the life of [name] and for kissing their forehead with your unconditional love. As you kiss their forehead, you awaken within them a great peace that moves over their whole being and washes through their heart.

It feels good to see [name] as a being of unconditional love, expressing and receiving the light of this world. Thank you for surrounding them in complete safety, for helping them to feel safe and for reminding them they are a light in this world.

I say this for the highest good and under the spiritual Law of Grace.

And so it is!

Silencing Nightmare Thoughts

When we've initiated healing, there's a chance that our ego voice will try and hold us back by bringing nightmare thoughts and fear-based memories to the forefront of our mind. But when we're faced with darkness, we're presented with an opportunity to be embraced by light once more. There comes a moment when we can choose either the madness mindset or the miracle mindset. Obviously, I'd suggest the miracle mindset!

The reason I call thoughts that I don't consider positive 'nightmares' is because, in the same way that a child who's had a bad dream is always told by a loving parent that it wasn't real, when I have a thought that's challenging and prepares me for the worst, I remind myself, 'It's only a nightmare, it's not real!' Then I follow my spiritual process to shift my perceptions.

My own process includes visualization techniques and meditation, but I know these can be challenging for many, so here are some other things (and beings) that may help you:

Archangel Michael

A simple prayer to Michael, the archangel and saint of protection, is sometimes the most accessible and effective form of safety. Michael is a huge archangel and I'm guessing you've already felt, encountered or called on him in your spiritual practice. Most of us have a strong image of this warrior-like angel protecting us.

Through the years Michael has been seen with a sword of light that he uses to disconnect us from anything that's not serving our life or purpose, and that includes negative and nightmare thoughts. You can call on him to clear your mind of the ego voice and its master plan to challenge your perception with this prayer:

'Thank you, Archangel Michael, for drawing close at this time and using your sword of light to disconnect me from thoughts, emotions and perceptions that are not serving my purpose of being aligned with happiness.

I surrender into your energy of protection and allow you to be the gatekeeper in my mind. I know that as you stand strong with your loving presence in my mind, you will only allow thoughts that serve, guide and protect me on my pathway to peace, happiness and love.

It's so good to know you're here with me.

And so it is!'

Cherub Angels

A recent thing that has become fun for me is the idea of cherub angels. There's actually a tier in the angelic hierarchy that includes beings called Cherubim. They are the angels who direct the divine will. In spiritual texts they've been described as having four wings and four faces, but in my practice I like to imagine them as the sweet little cherubs shown in Renaissance art.

When I'm having challenging thoughts or nightmare visions, I imagine that these happy, smiling little directors of the divine are dancing around me. I hold the vision that cherub angels of happiness are kissing me, stroking my hair and guiding me to let go of the disturbing thoughts that weren't real to begin with, until the thoughts have gone and I'm sharing the happiness of the cherub angels.

Flowers

For some reason, I've come to love flowers. When I was growing up, my mum had really challenging hay fever, so they were never really a part of my life. But once during a meditation I was given a sunflower by my guardian angel, Kamael, and since then it's been one of my spiritual symbols. Anytime I've found it difficult to surrender to a situation, I've visualized sunflowers. Sometimes I'll imagine the famous *Sunflowers* painting by van Gogh, but in my mind the flowers are happier-looking and even more colourful. Other times I'll imagine a sunflower with a big, happy, smiling face in the centre, gazing down on me.

I constantly change my spiritual practice, but I'm consistent in the sense that I'll go to something that feels familiar and safe when it comes to changing my perceptions. This is my 'safety process'.

Another flower I love is the daisy. I imagine I'm a wee boy running through a bright green field of grass with daisies all around me. Whenever I do that, the joy of my inner child is brought to the surface like magic.

Loving Thoughts

It's important while following the steps of forgiveness to find your love and to stay connected with it. The people, pets, things, memories and parts of your community that make you feel included, safe, accepted and happy are important for your journey. Do you have childhood memories that make you ecstatic? What experience in the last 12 months has made you feel fulfilled and supported? Who brightens up your day?

Take some time in contemplation to cultivate a miraculous mindset by remembering only loving thoughts. When you're faced with a challenge, how can you make yourself feel safe and return to love? Take a moment to figure out your own safety process.

Remember that forgiveness isn't an action – it's a process of remembering your spiritual identity and your connection to love.

Chapter 7
THE BODY IS A TEMPLE

'The body can be healed as an effect of forgiveness.'
'THE SONG OF PRAYER', *A COURSE IN MIRACLES*

In order for the miracle of forgiveness to work its way through our life, it needs to be a full-body process. Our body is the home of our soul right now and it's really important to keep that space clean and looked after.

Ever since my teenage years I've been fascinated by the connection between body and mind and how the spirit dwells between them. I've also been intrigued by the fact that the way we treat our body is the way we see our true essence. And I've been blown away knowing that how people see their soul is how their body becomes. There's no doubt about it: our body needs forgiveness, too.

A Course in Miracles teaches that we are much more than our body – in fact, we're much more than this Earth. And it's true! But – and that's a big *but* – we're here right now, we're here on Earth and we're here in a body, so we need to respect that and make the journey as comfortable as possible.

The truth is that how we treat our body is how we treat our soul. That's something to really contemplate. Learning it has been one of my biggest challenges. For years I honestly shunted off every act of self-care for my body because I thought all the spiritual stuff was going to do it for me. What was I thinking?

Learning that we have a body, a mind *and* a soul is important. They are like three best friends – they're all a bit different, but for some reason they go together well. Imagine one has a bigger butt, one thinks too much and one is off floating around and being all golden – that's your body, mind and soul!

Forgiveness is a process of spiritual integration – it helps us bring together mind, body and soul. It doesn't mean we'll end up a size 6, or have a quiet mind, or work as an energy healer (though we might), but it does mean we'll have love and respect for every part of our being.

Forgiveness in the body allows us to feel differently about a situation and it lets us be real. Have you ever noticed when someone's lying? Their body says it all – they just can't hide it. I believe that when we don't forgive, our body tells that story, too.

A Holy Temple

The way I look at it is simple: our body is a beautiful temple. It's the home of our soul. But, like all beautiful spaces, if we leave it untended for a while, it can change very quickly. Think of an old church – the paint can chip off the wall, the wood can warp, smells, dust and bugs can take over the space and very quickly what was once beautiful can become unkempt and unloved.

Our body is *exactly* the same. When we don't allow forgiveness to take place, it's as though we lack love for ourselves. Then we allow the home of our soul to get spoiled and dusty – things don't shine like they once did.

Forgiveness is like *feng shui* – it's the cleanout that's needed, and once that's taken place, it's surprising how things change. When we begin to move forgiveness through our life, our body will begin to reflect acceptance and trust.

Louise Hay is one of my biggest inspirations, not only because she created my publisher, but because of the healing she has created in her life and the world. Louise's well-known book *You Can Heal Your Life* has become a bible to me and a vital part of my spiritual practice, particularly when it comes to working with family, friends and, of course, my clients. From it, I learned that how we feel inside can be reflected in our body and a lot of challenging, unforgiving and resentful thoughts can manifest as a physical condition. Since then I've worked with countless people, including myself, on changing thoughts and feelings, and then have seen them reflected in changes in the body.

Embracing Change

As I said previously, from early on, my weight was always a challenge for me. I resolved it through changing the way I felt about myself and forgiving myself for getting to that stage to begin with, but the journey wasn't over just like that. When I began to lose weight, I changed something else too, an old habit actually, that brought another opportunity to heal and forgive.

You're probably going to cringe when you read this (but that's cool): I used to be addicted to fizzy drinks. I totally loved them – I could drink up to six cans of pop every day! The amount of sugar in those cans was crazy. So, when I started my health plan, I switched to diet drinks. But I was still drinking up to six cans a day.

Everything was fine – at first. Then something strange began to happen: when I worked out, if I got too hot, or just randomly sometimes, a rash would appear all over my body.

I'd be so angry and itchy, I'd get all flustered and agitated. And this went on for months.

I don't know why I didn't do it sooner, but eventually I consulted the angels. I went into my bedroom, lit a red candle and sat cross-legged in front of my altar. Breathing deeply and locking my eyes shut, I began to pray: 'Thank you, angels, for reminding me of your presence and for drawing close today in my meditation practice. It's so good to have you here.'

I began to relax and just let the experience be. In my mind I began to see my guardian angel, Kamael, and my forgiveness angel, Joel, in front of me. They appeared in the form of light instead of their normal human forms. I smiled in my mind, but also with my body, because I knew how much I was loved.

I said to them, 'Thank you, guys, for being here and for revealing what I need to know about my skin rash.'

Instantly, as clear as day, I heard a single word: 'Aspartame.'

It was a lightbulb moment.

I remember thanking the angels for giving me the message loud and clear. I stayed in their presence for a while, just receiving healing from their light. It was a beautiful moment. When it was over, I said, 'Thank you,' and opened my eyes. It's funny – when I close my eyes and connect to the angels it feels more real than when I open my eyes and come back to Earth!

After the experience, I took some time to process what had happened. I realized that there was work to be done – I was embarking on a process, healing an addiction. I remembered that there were 12 cans of Diet Irn-Bru (Scotland's luminous orange national soft drink) chilling in the fridge, but I was ready to let them go. I kept saying the Louise Hay affirmation 'I am willing to change' and from that day on I quit drinking aspartame-filled drinks. My addiction was over and it wasn't creeping back in.

When I told my mum, she said, 'I told you to stop drinking so much of that stuff, but you didn't want to listen.'

She was right – she *had* told me. It's funny when it comes to guidance – angels will often encourage our loved ones and close friends to be their voice. Most of the time we probably won't realize it, and neither will they, but there's a chance that when we think a loved one's being critical, they're really bringing us guidance from above.

Is a family member encouraging you to give up an old habit concerning food, cigarettes or something else? And do you feel they're right, but find it hard to hear? These people are being the messengers of the divine and of your body – they're giving you an opportunity to remember love and to forgive.

It took a few weeks for the rash to die down, but soon I wasn't itching and scratching all the time. Every now and then something would trigger it again, though – like the day I was eating chewing gum and started to get itchy and the next minute my whole body was covered. Yes, aspartame was in it too!

It went on like this for months – every time I had something with that harsh chemical ingredient in it, the rash would flare up. I became really pernickety about the small print on everything I consumed, screwing up my eyes and trying to work out the wee letters. Over time I moved on to organic candy and soft drinks and dark chocolate. I found aspartame-free gum for when I wanted to chew something. I continued on and I really thought that it was over – the healing was done. But it wasn't.

After a while, the rash started coming back, but this time it was heat-related. If I was working out in the gym or part of a really strong yoga class, my body would react to my sweat or to the heat I was generating.

The rash was back, and with a vengeance. It really rocked my confidence. I'd just lost 65lbs and I was feeling much better about my physical body – what had I missed?

Holiday Healing

I was due to go on holiday with my friends Scott and Sean – we were off to Mallorca for a week of fun in the sun. All three of us are big fans of club music and we love going to see some of the world's biggest DJs live, so we were counting down the days to the trip.

Just a few weeks before we were due to set off, my body was in a state – my rash was as big as ever and it was recurring. I prayed for help and used affirmations to clear up my skin, but there was no joy. I remember feeling so ashamed and so frustrated by my body: why was it doing this to me?

After long chat, my mum and I decided that the doctor was the only option. Anyone who knows me will realize that was a last resort. I don't do doctors, or hospitals, if I can, because I really believe in our ability to heal ourselves. And I say that having spent months in hospital as a child.

I made an appointment and was able to see my doctor within the week. It was a weird experience because I hadn't seen him since I was at school. Not surprisingly, he'd got older and had some grey hairs. He was nice, gave me time to speak and, after looking at my skin, announced: 'It's urticaria.'

'What does that mean?'

The doctor told me that my skin was highly sensitive (just like the rest of me then) and that he could give me an anti-histamine to help calm it down, so I decided to surrender to the whole process and accept his prescription. I took the (huge) tablets immediately – I just wanted to see if they would help.

I think they did work at first. But as soon as we were on holiday, the rash started up again. Every time I went to take off my top, it crept up and started blotching up huge pink hives all over my body. I was so embarrassed. I was blessed to have two good pals with me, though, because they put soothing cream on areas of my back I couldn't reach and would tell me if they could see the rash coming up my neck. I didn't let it ruin the holiday and once my skin acclimatized to the weather, humidity and heat change, it did settle down.

We had a great time in Mallorca and there weren't any disagreements or anything – we all just had the best time. I was the explorer of our trio, while the boys liked a good lie-in until three in the afternoon, ha, ha.

Still, the rash needed my attention and I couldn't work out why it was there – well, I *could*, but I didn't know if I was willing to admit it. In my spiritual practice I'd learned that skin challenges represented feeling 'safe' or 'comfortable' in your own skin, and even though I'd transformed how I looked and felt, I still didn't fully accept myself.

It took another eight months before I really healed the issue and in the end it was a natural progression of my spiritual path. As I moved through my yogic practice, strengthening my body and mind every day and becoming more focused and flexible, I decided that taking up hot yoga would be cool. I'd heard some amazing things about it and how it could take your practice much further. My friend Stephen had told me about his aunt's new studio in Glasgow, called Infinity, and I decided that I would check it out.

'It's Getting *Hot* in Here'

My first night at hot yoga had come. Stephen's aunt, Colette, was teaching the class. I was really excited because the reviews online were brilliant and I learned that she was a senior yoga teacher with over 20 years' experience. I remember wearing a light T-shirt and my favourite cotton yoga shorts to the class. The room was full, with around 30 people side by side looking in the mirror. It was also roasting and I was going to be in there for 90 minutes!

Colette came in. She was high energy and she remembered everyone's name – and I mean *everyone*. You'd hear her give us the pose, then go, 'Sam, heel down. Lola, chest open. Jamie, keep going – push more – good correction!' I was absolutely amazed!

The only way to describe the class was exhilarating. I've never sweated so much in my life. The heat was crazy. It was nearly 40°C (100°F) but, with copious amounts of water and encouragement, I managed to work my way through the series of flowing, standing and seated postures.

Upon leaving the class I felt unstoppable. I had a smile from ear to ear. It was exactly the kind of class I'd been looking for and I was definitely going to do a lot more of it. I changed my clothes and made my way home for a long bath – but when I got home I realized I was covered in a rash.

I didn't want this to be the end of my new hobby already. After a chat with my mum, who thought it could have been down to too much sweat coming out of my body, I decided I was keeping up the yoga whatever. I'd booked another session only two days later and I went to it regardless.

After that, I went three or four times a week. I loved it so much and I started to get to know everyone who worked there. And for some reason I couldn't help but be the one who did something silly in class. One night I was doing standing bow, a pose that encourages you to hold a foot from behind while standing on the other one and leaning forwards so you look like a dancer, and Jamie, who was teaching that night, said, 'Kick that foot back,' and I ended up kicking so hard, I kicked him! The whole class was laughing when he then announced, 'I didn't mean "Kick *me*", Kyle!'

Sometimes I'd have to lie down and take a break while everyone else was practising, though. I often overheated. I felt suffocated, to be honest. My top would always be drowning me because it became heavy and sticky once it was covered in sweat.

I decided to have some private sessions with Colette because I'd come to really love and respect her style of teaching and I knew she could help me to improve my balance. During one of our sessions I told her about my concerns about overheating in class and she came up with a solution.

I remember that day so well. We were bang centre in the middle of the studio, speaking about my balance and moving through the postures of Absolute, my favourite sequence in hot yoga. I mentioned to Colette that I found the hot classes challenging and felt that my top was suffocating me and she said, 'Well, just practise without a top then – simple!'

I looked at her, puzzled.

'You've absolutely nothing to be embarrassed about,' she went on. 'I mean, who are you doing yoga for?'

I replied, 'Me!' and the penny suddenly dropped.

Shifting Perspective

At that moment it dawned on me that my ego voice had been so loud, telling me that everyone would be looking at my body and how scared it was of that, especially as I had more chest than your average man, that it had drowned out that fact that I was there for *myself*. And so was everyone else. Most people in a hot yoga class were going to be more bothered about dealing with the heat, staying hydrated and getting their posture right than anything else. They certainly weren't going to be bothered about me or my body.

I decided to go home that night and meditate – I was finally ready to be comfortable in my own skin, and more than that, I was willing to forgive myself for putting myself through such persecution.

Sitting on my bed, I closed my eyes, called on my angels and thanked them for being with me at that time. I then visualized the energy of Mary Magdalene behind me. As she began to wash her beautiful ruby-red light over my body from head to toe, internally I said something along the lines of:

'My body is a temple and I honour it now.

There is no place safer than my own body.

My skin glows radiant and strong,

Love surrounds me, love is within me.

The light of unconditional love moves through my hair, skin and bones.

Thank you, angels, for helping me see the miracle that is my body.

I am safe here. I am safe.

And so it is!'

Something happened within that practice, because I felt as though I was wide open and blessed. I remember standing in front of my mirror in my bedroom with my T-shirt off, just honouring my body and embracing it for what it was. This skin was holy and I was honouring my temple because I finally realized it was the home of my soul.

I knew the theory already, I knew the words, but this time it was for real. The energy of self-acceptance through forgiveness flowed through me. I'd allowed forgiveness to be a full-body experience. It had gone skin deep.

I remember my first ever class after that session. Jamie was teaching again. It was a Saturday, 10 a.m., Absolute sequence. I was greeted at the desk with warm smiles and after having my card stamped and collecting fresh towels, I headed off to the changing room. I had a pair of shorts and a vest just in case, but I knew exactly what I needed to do. I pottered around longer than usual, then decided that was it: I was just wearing shorts! I headed into the class.

On my way there I saw Jamie and said, 'I'm doing it topless today!'

He smiled, saying, 'Yer out and yer proud – let's have a great class!'

It was just what I needed to hear.

The class *was* great and I felt completely *free*. I didn't even think about what anyone might be thinking of me because I was too busy working on my practice. I didn't overheat and I felt absolutely focused. I just remember reaching relaxation and the end of the class and releasing all the fear from my body – it was over, the forgiveness was complete.

Practising hot yoga topless became a thing. It became part of my ritual to go into class without my vest on. But a few weeks had passed before I realized something completely miraculous: my rash had disappeared. By then I was practising yoga five or six times a week and had even started to run in the gym again, and, yep, you've guessed it, no rash.

I believe that my body had not only learned how to deal with temperature changes because of the heated room but on a deeper level my skin had accepted forgiveness as I'd stepped into my power and honoured who I really was and the amazing changes I'd made both inside and out. I was healed.

'I Thought He Was Good!'

A while ago I received this lovely e-mail from a girl who needed to realize that lack of forgiveness was affecting her whole life, including her body. Here's what she said:

Hi, Kyle,

I bought your Angel Prayers book and with it you sent me the 'Forgiveness' card. I'll admit that at the time I thought, Pfft, I thought he was good, obv. not, as at that point, I thought it only meant forgiving other people and no one had done me wrong.

In the last few months, though, I realized it was myself I had to forgive, as I had given up on everything I was doing. My business was failing, I was grumpy all the time, never played with my gorgeous girls and was gaining weight at an alarming rate, but I just didn't care, I felt that I just failed at everything I tried to do. Then I was walking through Central station a few months ago (I'm never in Central usually) and we actually bumped into each other. I don't expect you to remember that, lol, but it inspired me to re-read your book and that card fell out again. Then it hit me! I wasn't miserable because I was failing – I was failing because I was miserable! So I had a good look at what I had done wrong and I let it all go. I released myself from any past guilt and decided to move forwards.

I have taken a totally new career path which is making me happier, I have started playing squash and joined jogscotland, and the girls and I in the last month have spent more time playing than anything else. I'm so grateful for everything that has changed – and all from that card I thought you'd got wrong!

Now I want to come to see you for a private session!

Love

Lynsey

Tooth vs Truth

A year or so ago I saw a boy I knew posting constantly online about the toothache he had. He just couldn't get it to go away. He was in so much pain that he couldn't sleep and it was affecting his work.

Callum was in a band, but not only that, he had a day job in insurance too, so he needed all the energy he could get. I decided that I'd offer my help if he was open to it. I knew that it wasn't right to force your ideas down people's throats (quite literally, you'll soon learn), but he'd recently expressed some interest in meditation and other things I like to post about, such as the tarot, so I sent him a private message.

He instantly replied, 'I'll try anything. I've had the strongest painkillers and nothing is taking this pain away – I'd love your insight, man. Thanks!'

In spirituality the mouth is governed by the throat chakra *(see page 117)* and it represents our ability to speak our truth. If we're not honest about something, energy can fester in that area of the body. I knew from seeing a client in the past that toothache, in particular, was to do with a painful truth that you didn't want to come to terms with.

I decided that it was too much to throw all of this at Callum straightaway, but if I could just give him an affirmation on speaking the truth, maybe he'd get the point. I sent him a copy of Louise Hay's affirmation for teeth:

I make my decisions based on the principles of truth, and I rest securely, knowing that only right action is taking place in my life.

The next day Callum posted all over Facebook that he'd had a cure for his toothache from me. He said it was 'complete magic' and that he'd been able to get his first full night's sleep in days. Later he told me he'd been using the affirmation every day and things had begun to change in his life – so much so that he had to give me an update.

It turned out that he and his girlfriend had felt for months that their relationship wasn't working, but neither of them had been able to find the strength to tell the other. Not only that, Callum had found himself attracted to someone else and had had relations with another girl and the whole situation had been 'eating him up for months' – interesting, right? What do you eat with? The teeth and the mouth.

Unforgiving resentful thoughts can so easily harbour themselves as physical ailments in our body and fester away, especially if we refuse to deal with them. I was glad to be of service in this instance and was overjoyed to hear that both Callum and his girlfriend had found themselves new partners and moved on.

Body Care

I remember another beautiful experience when I worked with a girl privately. She had come because she wanted to see where her life was going, but she got a lot more than she bargained for.

I remember that when Jade walked in, there was a lightness to her aura colours. She seemed like a successful young girl. She had long, straight black hair and a slim figure. She was wearing mostly white and her top was yellow. By the build-up of energy around her tummy, I knew that she'd changed a lot in her life.

I also knew as soon as I saw her that she had a special connection with children – she was a teacher. She confirmed this and told me that she had retrained three years before.

When I was holding Jade's hands on top of my trusted angel cards, I knew that there was a need for self-forgiveness and that it was to do with her past eating habits. I could feel that Jade was dedicated to her work and doing well but still had major hang-ups around her body. Her body craved her forgiveness and her acceptance.

When I was shuffling the cards, I wasn't surprised that the 'Body Care' card flipped out and landed facing upwards. Jade looked at it and began to well up. She was realizing why she was sitting in my office.

An angel came and stood behind her. I wished I was wearing sunglasses – he was just *so bright*! I told Jade that a healing angel had arrived in the room and that he was there to guide her through a full-body forgiveness.

Then I began to speak clearly about her life – it was as though the angel had unloaded, or downloaded, this direct information right into my mind.

'Your angel wants you to know that he's so pleased that you've changed your old eating habits and that you've taken steps towards healing your life. He's so happy that you no longer make yourself sick or starve yourself of food when your body craves it. You've come so far and you've now begun to reap the benefits of being healthier. But still you feel challenged by energy and you have unreleased anger inside your belly, so you find it difficult to process food. It's as if your body can't let go and you feel frustrated. You feel fat, even though you know you're not, and you feel tired because of the heaviness in your belly.'

'How do you know all this?' Jade blurted out, her teardrops falling onto my matt-black desk.

'I don't – your angel does!'

I already knew that the solar plexus, the stomach area, was the seat of anger and frustration. I'd also found out, through years of practice, that when someone was angry about something and couldn't let go of their 'crap', they literally found it difficult to digest their food and then physically let go when they were in the loo.

I explained the energetic connections behind constipation and feeling 'bagged up' to Jade, and it struck a chord with her.

'You have an opportunity to heal your past for good today,' I told her, as she grabbed a large bundle of tissues and wiped the tears from her face. 'You've let go of the bad habits and you've begun to love yourself enough to eat, but the real question is this: are you willing to forgive yourself and your body for holding on to the past?'

'Yes! I'm ready!'

In the moments that followed, I saw a real shift in Jade. I could see her letting go on an energetic level as her guardian angel danced and swirled around her, clearing away the past. She had moved into a state of forgiveness and her body was energetically clearing away what was no longer serving her or her path to happiness.

We thanked the angels together and I helped her to see how her life would be moving forwards once the past had been cleared. I could see from her smiles and the change in her face that her external image was now definitely reflecting the lightness she was feeling inside.

When the session was wrapped, I knew that Jade was moving into a new space and later on I wasn't surprised to receive an e-mail of thanks telling me she was finally free both emotionally and physically.

I wrote myself a note on all of this here at 25,000 feet on a flight from Orlando, Florida, to JFK, New York:

Embodied

Your reality is not your body.
The truth of who you are is more than physical,
*   your reality is soul.*

You are pure spirit contained within a body.
Your body is the home of your soul, the seat in which your
*   holiness sits.*

In order for forgiveness to become 'real', it needs to become
*   embodied.*
Forgiveness is remembering that you are whole already –
*   which extends to the skin you are in.*

Imagine a beautiful temple,
dressed in gold and filled with light.
At the heart of the temple rests a throne.
In front of the throne an altar is laid.
Upon the altar is the divine,
the source of creation.

Your body is that holy temple,
the altar is your mind
and the seat of the divine is your heart.
The temple is incomplete without the altar.
An altar is bare without its source.

Forgiveness needs to be embodied.
Spirit requires integration.
A sense of community must be cultivated within.
Acceptance of your wholeness must extend to the tips of your
*   fingers and toes.*
Unity begins when you remember the divine rests here,
*   within you!*
Holiness is restored when you open your eyes and see.

A Ritual Bath

I know in this day and age it's a shower world, but I've found that some of my most profound healing thoughts and inspirations have come to me in the bath. As this chapter is all about cultivating the awareness that your body is the temple of your soul, it would be beautiful for you to spend some time with your body integrating with your soul essence. So why not have a bath?

Preparing a ritual bath is easy – you just have to create a beautiful space and use something that helps you to feel that you can nourish your body and connect with the real inner you.

For my ritual baths I combine 10mls of organic absolute rose oil with 100mls of organic apricot oil. I usually leave it to blend and the bottle lasts a good six months or so, used sparingly in the bath.

I then light candles all around the bath and get in.

When I'm in, I allow the oils to kiss my skin and then massage them into it, allowing it to be nourished and loved. As I lie there naked, I feel free and know that at that moment I am one with my body and soul.

You can prepare a ritual bath using oils, too, and here are some other suggestions as well:

✧ Allow your favourite crystals to soak in the water before you enter the bath.

✧ Put rose petals on top of the water (another personal favourite).

✧ Use Himalayan pink salt to bless the water.

✧ Light your favourite incense in the bathroom.

✧ Put on a face mask before entering the bath.

✧ Play your favourite love songs while you lie in the bath.

✧ Have a loved one give you a massage in the bath or wash your back or hair for you.

✧ Do whatever makes you feel loved, nourished and sensual.

Chapter 8
THE WHEELS OF FORGIVENESS

'Your holy mind establishes everything that happens to you.'

Chakra is a Sanskrit word that means 'wheel' and is used to describe the spiritual projections of the soul into the physical body. I have written about the chakras in my previous books, but felt that it was important to explain how forgiveness moves through the spiritual energy field, so here is a little more on these 'wheels of forgiveness'.

Whether the chakras are 'real' or not doesn't bother me, because they give us a map to work with and that's the important thing. This map is of our spiritual self and how it manifests in our life on a physical and emotional level.

There are seven major chakras (and a lot more minor ones) and they are related to the physical parts of our body and how they serve our spiritual function in life. These seven centres are like doorways – they have to do with how we receive energy and how we express it.

I believe that when we have unforgiving energy in our life, it *may* manifest on a physical level and in an energetic sense it can build up in a particular chakra. When we move into forgiveness, the energy is released and sent out into our life, and it gives our soul permission to begin the healing on an external level. It's actually quite fascinating to see. Here's an outline of the chakras, how resentment and unforgiving and stubborn thoughts can manifest in them and how we can shift our perceptions to change our body on a physical and emotional level.

Our chakras start at the base of our spine and move upwards to the crown of our head. Our energy manifests at the base of our spine and moves upwards, too. Understanding how it works is easy. Think of a hose moving water along a sprinkler system. The hose is plugged into the water supply and there are seven sprinklers being fed from it. If the start of the hose has a leak, all the sprinklers will be affected – and it's exactly the same with the chakras. Energy can move up and down through our energy centres, but it's when they are all balanced and functioning correctly that they reach their maximum potential.

Chakras are like little doorways or portals – they open and close naturally as we move through different experiences. There's a lot out there about balancing our chakras or clearing them, but there's very little on consciously opening them. In my spiritual practice if there's an area of my life that needs balancing, or even just some attention, I put my focus on the relevant chakra, work through forgiveness in that area and allow that chakra to open, because it's then that its energy will materialize in my life.

Here are the chakras.

The Base Chakra: *Muladhara*

Muladhara is a Sanskrit word that means 'root support' and this chakra is found at the base of our spine. It is connected to the energy surrounding what we rely on as our 'backbone' in the physical world. On a physiological level, it has to do with the base of the spine, the pelvis, the legs and the feet. The colour that represents it is a beautiful red.

The energy of this centre affects and is affected by:

- our physical health
- our community and close ones
- our home and security
- our grounding

If our base chakra were in nature, it would be the soil in which seeds are planted. It's the foundation in which everything is planted. That's why it's important to be aware of this chakra. It's the area of my life I constantly check in with – in fact, I wear the symbol of the base chakra on my wrist and I *never* take it off.

When the energy of the base chakra gets blocked, it can cause a whole lot of challenges because this is the chakra that feeds the others their energy. If this area of your world needs attention, address it first, before progressing any further. Sort out any issues here first.

We've all met a person who walks around stooped over as if they're carrying the weight of the world on their shoulders, haven't we? It's quite crazy if you think of it, but this is what happens when so much energy has built up in the base chakra that it's begun to fester and cause issues.

It's interesting that most people who have bad backs have issues with security, home, family or the ability to stay grounded. These areas of their life need their attention, but they keep putting it off – and at the same time they're allowing themselves to suffer even more.

Forgiveness through the base chakra helps us come to an acceptance of our foundation in life – how it has made us the person we are and how we can grow from that space.

The base chakra energy challenges us to stand our ground in a loving way, taking on aspects of life that serve us, and reminds us that it's OK to say 'no' when we can't be of service to others. It's when we can't look after our own security or when we put everyone else's first that this centre can become stuck or leak energy.

This energy centre calls us to release ideas of lack and limitation – it reminds us that we live in a sustainable world where we can manifest the means to provide for ourselves and our close ones.

The element that rules this chakra is earth and we can empower the chakra simply by connecting to this element through Mother Nature.

Forgiveness and the Base Chakra

Before opening this centre to allow any build-up of energy to be released and to encourage to flow of balance through your life, it's important to review any areas of your life linked with this chakra that require your forgiveness.

Your Foundation

Think of your community, loved ones and family. Are there areas of this world where you could work on forgiveness? Were your parents absent? Was there a lack of financial support or security as you were growing up? Was a parent (or both parents) missing altogether? This is your foundation.

The angels who govern the base chakra draw close when you prepare to open this centre and remind you that this is the soil of your life. When you look around you, you can see how others planted the seeds of their lives and how they allowed the flowers to blossom. This is your chance to prepare your foundation in order to plant the seeds of what happens next in your life.

Your Health

If your health has challenged you throughout your life or you're going through something with your physical body right now, it's important to figure out if there's any resentment or frustration around that area that's been left unaddressed.

The angels of the base chakra remind you that you have every right to be here on Earth and nothing can take that away from you. These beautiful angels with a ruby-red aura help you to remember that your body responds to your mental-spiritual self and by taking the time to remember your spiritual wholeness, you encourage your physical body to reflect that.

Connect with the Earth

Now that you've worked through the base chakra areas that require your forgiveness, you have a beautiful opportunity to offer the resistance of forgiveness to the element that this chakra represents. The angels of the earth and of the base chakra will manifest around you as you work through this process and help you to move through it.

You don't have to go outdoors for this (especially if that's not doable for you at this time), but I'd recommend it if you can. Go somewhere and connect with nature – maybe sit on the grass or the sand or in the woodlands and breathe in the beautiful planet we live on. Just draw the Earth itself closer and closer with every breath. If thoughts run through your head, just allow them to float in and out of it – allow yourself to be held by the mother who is below you.

Spend as much time doing this as you need. I always find it helpful (while sitting down) to place my hands at either side of my hips and push down, creating a straight spine, and I then allow all resistance to move from my hands into the ground. I see in my mind the Earth turning the resistance into soil and allowing it to be used for the growth of other living beings.

Here's a prayer:

'Thank you, Mother Earth and angels of the planet, for bringing me energy that provides a sense of balance, groundedness and security.

At this time I allow my base chakra to release all resistance to forgiveness in the areas of my life that make me question my physical health, my security, my community, loved ones and my family.

I now accept the balancing energy of earth and allow it to move into my base chakra, the point in my body that keeps me strong, rooted and connected to everything that is in perfect harmony.

I am grateful for this balance. I am safe here in my body and I allow this centre to open and move in the ways that are best for my path.

And so it is!'

The Sacral Chakra: *Svadisthana*

Svadisthana is a Sanskrit word that means 'one's own place' and this chakra is found around our pubic bone and above our navel. It is connected to how we flow with life and how much trust we have in it. As this is an area that deals with trust, it also has to do with the most sacred aspect of our body and life: our sexuality. On a physical level, it has to do with our genitals, our reproductive system – inside and out. The colour that represents the sacral area is a bright orange.

The energy of this centre affects and is affected by:

- our sexuality and sexual health
- our relationships
- our reproductive system
- our finances
- how we flow with life

If our sacral chakra were in nature, it would be the water that feeds the soil in which our seeds are planted. It has a large role to play in the nurturing and sustaining of life.

When the energy of the sacral chakra gets blocked, it can affect so much of our life, in particular our relationship with ourselves. This may happen when we ignore our sexual self. This is something that many of us are embarrassed to talk about – it's as though we're ashamed of who we are! We become locked inside ourselves, scared to show our true colours, and our sacral chakra becomes imbalanced and sends our sexual desires all over the place.

But we are sexual beings – in fact, without sex, we wouldn't exist – and it's so important to cherish this aspect of ourselves. Sexual moments can be considered spiritual, whether they are with someone we love or on our own.

The sacral chakra is the centre of the spiritual anatomy that allows us to be at home with ourselves. It's the energy centre that wants us to see that we are a sexual being and that sex is a beautiful thing, especially when we treat it in a respectful way.

It's interesting that when a person has had a challenging sexual experience in their life, the pattern seems to repeat itself. I've met many people through my practice who've been used sexually in relationships or, even worse, been abused on that level, and it's repeated itself over and over. I've also found that an experience like this affects not only their relationships with others, but also with themselves. Most people who've been sexually abused or mistreated harbour the shame of it, sometimes to the point of blaming themselves for the experience. But forgiveness through the sacral chakra helps us to accept our sexual self and allows us to enter the inner temple.

The sacral centre helps us to remember that we should be respected and pleasured, but that we can give respect and pleasure, too. It challenges us and our relationships so that we can let go of the ones that aren't serving us and cherish the ones that are holy.

It also calls us to explore our spiritual-sexual self and helps us to see that these areas are connected. It calls us to see that the divine Creator can come into play within each woman and man. When this aspect of us is balanced and accepted, the rest of our life will begin to flow and be expressed with ease.

The element associated with the sacral centre is water, which may be surprising, especially because the colour associated with it is orange. The main reason is because the essences of reproduction are water-based and the fluid that sustains the embryo in the womb is surrounded by water.

There's also a great connection between our sexual self and our financial security, because they both reflect our fluidity – can we give and receive in perfect balance?

Forgiveness and the Sacral Chakra

Before opening up the sacral chakra and allowing any build-up of energy to come out, it's important to review the aspects of your life and spiritual growth that balancing this centre will change as well as the aspects of this chakra that need your forgiveness.

Your Sexual Self

Connecting with your sexual self is an important part of forgiveness and can be easily missed. Have you deprived yourself of sexual pleasure or have you been deprived by a partner? Has someone in your past mistreated you sexually? Do you feel that your sexual self is unexpressed? Have you had a miscarriage or an abortion, or been otherwise deprived of a child you created? Have you failed to share your sexuality with a close one? Or is your sex drive too high? Have you had (in your eyes) too many sexual partners? These are the areas this chakra calls you to review and forgive. Remember, you can't change the past, you can only change your attitude and where you are now.

The angels of the sacral chakra want you to know that when you're having an intimate moment that is genuine, either with yourself or with a partner, they rejoice because you're expressing who you are and nourishing a part of your human make-up that's easily forgotten.

Your Finances

The universe wants you to be financially secure in life. The energy of the sacral centre is connected to the infinite flow of abundance and it encourages you to accept it. If you've had financial challenges in the past or have them in the present, your sacral centre calls you to explore and forgive them now. Whether you've been in debt or you've inherited it, it's time to change how you view your finances. Whether you've felt too greedy or too needy, whether you've had too much or not enough, the sacral is spiralling out of control. Forgiveness will help you to express nourishment, balance and fluidity in finance.

Connect with Water

Vast, abundant and flowing, water is the element that governs the sacral chakra and restores its natural balance. Now that you've given some attention to the areas governed by this chakra and how you can work through them with forgiveness, it would be helpful to connect with the angels and the element of water to allow healing energy to flow through your life.

To connect with the element of water and encourage your sacral chakra to be open and receptive to the angels and to balancing energy, there are two things that I highly recommend. The first one is a bath. Put sea salt in it and immerse yourself in the warm, supportive energy. Allow yourself to be held by the natural element of water and allow its healing to unfold naturally.

The other option is standing with your feet in the sea. (Make sure it's safe to do so and if it's cold, look after your circulation.) Open your arms wide and just allow yourself to connect to its abundant energy.

Here's a prayer:

> 'Thank you, vast and abundant water and your angels, for bringing to me a healing, supportive and balancing wave of peace.
>
> At this time I allow my sacral centre to release all resistance to forgiveness in the areas of my sexuality, relationships and financial flow.
>
> I now accept the balancing energy of water and allow it to move into my sacral centre, the point in my body reminding me that within I hold a holy temple I can express through my spiritual and sexual self.

I am grateful to be free and flowing. It is safe to be who I am and I allow this centre to open and move in the ways that are best for my path.

And so it is!'

⁓

The Solar Plexus Chakra: *Manipura*

Manipura is a Sanskrit word that means 'lustrous gem' and this chakra is found in our tummy, above the navel. It is connected to our willpower and drive, and is fascinating because it's like a large sun in the centre of our body, shining bright yellow-gold. On a physical level, it has to do with our digestive system.

The energy of this centre affects and is affected by:

- our willpower
- our drive for success
- our vitality
- our digestive system

If our solar plexus chakra were in nature, it would be the sun that photosynthesizes the seeds planted in the soil and kept moist by the water. It is the fire energy that brings warmth and encourages the seeds to sprout and reach towards the light.

When the energy of the solar plexus chakra gets blocked, it can cause an intense amount of heat in the energy system that can make us angry, agitated and difficult to be around. Have you ever felt that you're about to explode with anger? Or that you're tired, you're rushing around and you're just too hot? Have you ever felt that the slightest thing could tick you off or, even worse, send you over the edge? On days like this, it seems that your solar plexus centre is about to explode, too – it's got so much energy building up, but it's not flowing!

Another thing that's interesting is that when you're feeling nervous about something, there's a good chance that your tummy will be swirling around like crazy. Your bowel can get irritable and can increase your visits to the loo – that's your solar plexus energy (*your willpower*) leaking right out.

When our solar plexus isn't aligned, our drive for success is depleted, as is our vital self. Forgiveness through the solar plexus chakra, on the other hand, helps us to let go when we feel we haven't done enough and assert our will when it comes to moving forwards.

The solar plexus is the area of our body that can hang on to so much we don't need – especially if we feel that we've failed in something. This energy centre challenges us to stop dwelling on past mistakes and see the light in our present, then draw more positive, uplifting experiences towards us.

The solar plexus calls on us to see that we create our own success by acknowledging where we stand today. It helps us to take in the sunshine of our life and really experience the warmth of the positive choices that we've made this far.

The element that rules this chakra is fire and we can empower this centre simply by connecting to this element through flames and heat.

Forgiveness and the Solar Plexus Chakra

Before unleashing the energy of your solar plexus, you must review the areas of your life where you feel drained and frustrated. Allow yourself to think differently about your choices and forgive your past mistakes with regards to your pathway, success and vitality before drawing down the energy of the sun so you can shine brightly again.

Your Willpower and Drive

It's really important to have a look at how you measure yourself and your success. If you feel that you've not worked hard enough or, even worse, been a total failure in this respect, then it's vital to shift your perceptions and create some healing. Seeing yourself as ineffective or powerless can really contribute to the challenges you're facing and it's important to know that you have a mighty source of power within to create positive changes in your life. Forgive yourself for past mistakes and for lack of drive – it's never too late for anything!

Your Vitality

If you've suffered, or are suffering, from a lack of energy and get frustrated because of it, it's time to change. Many people find it hard to believe, but health is our natural state. So your body is naturally healthy. When you're feeling tired, restless and all over the place, it's because there are other factors contributing towards your depletion.

In order to restore your vitality, you have to honour what your body's telling you. If you eat a meal or a particular type of food and instantly want to go to sleep when you finish it, or even during it, your body's telling you it doesn't like it. Forgive yourself for all the times you've ignored your body's natural signs and rhythms.

Connect with Fire

As the element of fire governs your solar plexus, you can burn away any resentful thoughts, energy and setbacks with its power. You can also call on the angels of fire and the angels of the sun (solar power) to bring the cleansing energy of forgiveness to your body and your whole life.

The easiest way to draw fire into your body is to enjoy the sunshine. Having a day in the warmth of the sun is a wonderful way to draw down all its healing qualities. When you get the time to spend relaxing in the sun, imagine its light shining down and moving into your belly. As it comes into you, see it miraculously clearing away any darkness, frustrations and anger, allowing you to clearly assert your will. As you know, the sun is a positive planet – it makes us feel so good when we've been out in its rays and it releases all the happy chemicals in our brain. Why not allow it to balance your spiritual anatomy?

Here's a prayer:

> 'Thank you, sun energy and solar angels, for sending down positive and uplifting vital life-force into my being.
>
> At this time I allow my solar plexus chakra to release all resistance to forgiveness concerning how well I've done with my goals up to this point. I now accept the inspirational energy of fire, knowing it will drive me forwards so that I can turn my personal goals into achievements.
>
> I realize my happiness isn't based on external achievements but on internal balance and I accept my natural state of wellness now. I am grateful for the inspiration of my angels and aim to inspire others, too. I am shining brightly as I spread my wings on this path.
>
> And so it is!'

The Heart Chakra: *Anahata*

The heart chakra is the centre of both the spiritual and physical anatomy. It's the space that we're all connected to but rarely acknowledge.

Anahata is a Sanskrit word that means 'unstruck', referring to the spiritual acceptance that the heart can never be broken. The heart chakra is associated with the colour green and also pink. On a physical level, it has to do with the heart, chest and respiratory system.

The heart centre affects and is affected by:

- altruism and service
- giving and receiving love
- our connection to love
- our heart muscle
- how we view ourselves

If our heart chakra were in nature, it would be the air that we breathe to keep ourselves alive. It would also be the air that carries the pollen from one plant to another and the air that they breathe.

When the energy of the heart centre gets blocked, it can disconnect us from our natural state of being loving and accepting support from others. We are beings of love and it is natural for us to express and receive love, but most of us allow one of these to dominate. In fact, we've all been on one side of the fence or the other. There are people who are so giving they'd cut their left arm off and hand it to someone and there are others who will just take, take, take!

The heart chakra is the centre that requires the most love to stay balanced, because it's the place where we feel everything the most. It's interesting that most people who are single or have challenges in relationships, either professional or personal, have had issues of being hurt, let down or betrayed in the past. It's almost as though the heart has been left unhealed and because of that has closed over and blocked off the TLC it deserves.

Forgiveness through the heart chakra helps us to move beyond heartbreak and into acceptance of our wholeness. It helps us to breathe deeply and exhale the sadness that is no longer serving our journey in love.

Heart chakra energy challenges us to balance the energy of love in our life. It tells us that it's OK to share the truth of who we are and that we can find the trust to welcome others into our world. As forgiveness takes place through the heart chakra, balance is brought to our ability to give and receive, and that's something that goes beyond just relationships.

This energy centre calls us to release the illusion that someone has taken all of our goodness and trust. It reminds us that it's natural for us to be in a state of love and to trust others, but only when we've come into balance with *ourselves.*

The element of this chakra is air and we can empower this centre simply by connecting to the beautiful fresh air of the outdoors or by burning incense.

Forgiveness and the Heart Chakra

Before opening the heart centre and allowing any build-up of hurt, resentment and unbalanced energy to be released, it's important to review the areas connected with the heart chakra that require your forgiveness.

Your Ability to Serve

Service is a natural aspect of the soul. To help, support and guide others is definitely a part of your divine spiritual purpose. However, this should not mean giving every aspect of yourself away. Service starts with yourself.

When you're bringing the healing power of forgiveness into your heart centre, it's important to say it's OK if you've put other people and their journey first. If there have been times when you've put others' needs before your own, it's time to forgive that now. Your angels want you to know that you did the best you could with the knowledge you had. But it's now time to serve yourself through forgiveness and a balanced life. When that's together, then you can serve others through your natural ability to be kind and loving.

Your Relationships

If you've felt challenged by your relationships, either with your parents or children or partner, now is your time to forgive. Your heart chakra can close over when you're holding in love or remembering how you were let down by another person. Recognizing that people only hurt each other when they've forgotten about love can help you to see why it's important to reopen your heart and let love flow.

The angels of relationships are coming to you at this time with their beautiful healing green aura and are helping you to recognize that your past relationship challenges do not determine your capacity to love or be loved. They are also helping you to see that the more you're able to love yourself and trust who you are, the more you're able to let others love you. Then you can form trust from that space.

Connect with the Air

Now that you've worked through any areas associated with the heart centre that may require your forgiveness, you've the perfect opportunity to release all resistance to this forgiveness. By allowing the element of air into your heart, you'll find the angels of the heart centre will help you to open your heart and restore your natural ability to give and receive love.

Going outdoors to meditate in the fresh air is idea. Make sure you settle down in a comfortable spot where there won't be many interruptions.

If going outdoors isn't practical for you at this time then there's a wonderful alternative: incense! Wrap up in a cosy blanket and light your favourite incense in a safe, fireproof space. You may want to use your hands to guide the smoke of the incense all over your body, especially to your heart centre.

Whether you're meditating outdoors or working with incense:

✧ Close your eyes.

✧ Allow the centre of your chest to expand as you inhale and then imagine you're breathing out anything that is no longer serving you on the exhale. Do this for a good 10–20 breaths.

✧ As I do this, I normally imagine breathing in light and then exhaling any darkness from my heart and body – representing expelling the negativity from my body. You may choose to do the same.

Here's a prayer:

'Thank you, angels of the heart and the element of air, for bringing healing and serenity to the centre of my being.

I allow my heart chakra to release all resistance to forgiveness in areas of my life that hold me back from giving and receiving love and experiencing trust. I now accept the balancing energy of air and allow it to move through my heart chakra, the point in my body that connects me to the oneness of every living being and the energy of unconditional love.

I am grateful for giving and receiving love in perfect love and perfect trust. I allow myself to be of service to all of humanity.

And so it is!'

The Throat Chakra: *Vishuddha*

Vishuddha is a Sanskrit word that means 'purification' and this energy centre is found in the throat and the thyroid gland. It is connected to the energy that allows us to express our creativity and speak our truth. The colour that represents this centre is light blue.

The energy of this centre affects and is affected by:

- our ability to be honest
- our creative abilities
- our emotions
- our voice

If our throat chakra were in nature, it would be the birds singing in the sky. To continue our plant analogy, it would be the space that holds the plant and allows it to flower.

When the energy of the throat centre gets blocked, it can cause a real sense of frustration. This is because the throat is where all our emotions are expressed. You'll know that from personal experience. If you're feeling emotional about something, you'll notice that your throat wants to close over or will feel clogged up.

We've all been overly emotional at one time or another. You and I both know what it's like when something's really bothering us. There's a sensation as though we're a volcano about to erupt and then energy moves right up our spine and begins coming out of us with a cry. Our sense of pain is expressed through our mouth: that is the throat chakra.

Conversely, this centre can become stuck or leak energy when we don't confess our true feelings about something, and that can stand between us and our creative self.

Forgiveness through the throat chakra helps us to accept who we really are and speak our truth. In the process, we are challenged to be honest with ourselves and others about who we are and where we want to go with it all.

So, the throat chakra calls us to release all ideas of non-acceptance and be true to ourselves. It encourages us to step into the spirit of integrity, the place where we are honest and real, but to honour others, too.

The element that rules the final three chakras – throat, third eye and crown – is space and we can empower all these centres by acknowledging the spaciousness within.

Forgiveness and the Throat Chakra

Before opening the throat chakra to allow any build-up of energy to be released and to bring in the balancing energy of space, it's important to review any areas of your life connected to this centre that will require your forgiveness.

Your Truth

Speaking our truth is so important, but sometimes being honest with others and ultimately ourselves is one of the hardest things to do. If this has been challenging for you in the past, the angels of the throat chakra are ready to help you forgive yourself now. If you feel that you should have told someone the truth about how you felt or you wish you'd told them who you really were but just couldn't, it's OK. It's also OK to be who you are. What's important is that you realize who you are and acknowledge it today. It's time to forgive yourself for not speaking up in the past. It's what you can change now that's important.

Your Creativity

Are you naturally creative? Do you have a special gift you want to express? If you feel frustrated because you've never done anything about it or upset because someone has stood between you and your creative self, now is the time to forgive and move forwards. Your angels want you to know that your creativity deserves the chance to shine but it can only do so if you move into a state of forgiveness. You see, when you have unforgiving energy in your throat chakra, only small aspects of your creative self can be expressed. But by taking the time to let go of any setbacks on your creative journey, you can bring all your creative energy into alignment with your soul.

Connect with Space

Now that you've allowed your spiritual self to be open, honest and creative and looked at the forgiveness aspects of that journey, it's time to release all resistance in your throat centre. The angels of space and of the throat chakra swirl around you now, helping you open and honour your divine self.

You're probably wondering how you connect with space, but don't worry, no NASA spaceship is required! Space is everywhere. It's the energy that moves through us, the aspect of the divine that's in the very atoms of our being.

To connect with space, you just need to move into a sense of silence, focusing on your breath and allowing yourself to be. Finding comfort in silence allows you to be one with all that is. I close my eyes and see the darkness of my eyelids and feel comforted there. I can't see anything, but that doesn't mean I'm alone. Just like in the movie *Avatar*, I see myself connecting to every living thing through the energy that ripples through me.

Here's a prayer:

> *'Thank you, angels of space, for entering into my heart and bringing me energy that gives a sense of freedom and acceptance.*
>
> *I allow my throat chakra to release all resistance to forgiveness in the areas of my life that stand between me and my truth and creativity. I now accept the balancing energy of space and allow it to move through my throat chakra, the point in my body that lets me to speak with integrity and show who I really am.*
>
> *I am so grateful for being able to express myself in an honest way.*
>
> *And so it is!'*

The Third Eye Chakra: *Ajna*

Ajna is a Sanskrit word that can be interpreted as 'perception' and the third eye chakra is found between the eyebrows. It's commonly known that this is the space that is connected to our vision, mind and psychic/spiritual awareness. The colour that represents it is indigo. On a physical level, it has to do with the eyes, ears and head.

The energy of this centre affects and is affected by:

- our perception
- how we see the world
- our intuition
- our psychic senses
- the clarity of our mind

If our third eye centre were in nature, it would actually go beyond it. It would be the divine intelligence that runs through the flower like ripples of energy and the guardian angel that protects it.

When the energy of the third eye chakra gets blocked, it can make us feel a little all over the place. The most common alert that we're blocked here is a sore head – it's almost as if all the energy in the environment we're in comes swooshing up our spinal column and builds up in our head.

The third eye can affect us in several ways. You know that feeling when all the pressure is building up in your head and all of a sudden you feel sick? Have you ever walked into a room and got all dizzy, only to find out something negative happened there in the past? Or, even worse, felt that someone was draining you? This is your third eye experiencing the energy of your surroundings.

Forgiveness through the third eye chakra helps us to change our perceptions completely. If we've judged or criticized someone who has done 'something bad' to us, there's a good chance we're allowing our third eye to get clogged up with negative energy. You see, when we point out something we don't like about someone, we're allowing that negative idea to taint our vision of their holiness, and the spiritual centre that is linked to our vision becomes tainted. When we move into forgiveness, on the other hand, our third eye opens and we're able to see the reality of spirit all around us.

This energy centre calls on us to release all harsh judgements and to move into a space where we trust what we feel and act upon it. It governs the psychic senses and has a close connection to the solar plexus centre. If we can trust what we feel and see the holiest in all sentient beings, our psychic vision will open up.

Forgiveness and the Third Eye Chakra

Before opening this centre to allow any build-up of psychic energy to be released, it's important to work out which areas linked to the third eye chakra need your forgiveness. Take a look at:

Your Perception

You have a choice about how you see the world around you. On the one hand, you can view it as a place filled with fear, negativity and challenges. This whole perception is based on fear, though, so if you choose this, you're likely to be living in a massive illusion.

Forgiveness through the third eye chakra helps you to heal this way of thinking so that you can choose to see the world based on love. In fact, it's time to release and forgive yourself for thinking negatively about the world you see and decide to see love everywhere you go. And when you choose to align your perception with the light in all beings, you'll allow your angels to draw closer than ever before.

Your Vision

Your vision of your life in your mind is most likely how it will be created in the world. Have you been through a negative experience that you expect to happen again? Do you get nervous about situation and then visualize the worst possible outcome just so you're prepared? It's time to forgive yourself for this and make a change. Your angels want you to know that it's always wise to think about the best possible outcome rather than the worst, because when you think of the best, you come into alignment with your highest good.

Connect with Spirit

Now that you've worked out which areas of your perception and vision can be changed and forgiven, you have the beautiful opportunity to draw the angels of spirit close to you. These angels will help you release all resistance to change so you can have a true sense of clarity. Remember, forgiveness is a state of being and as you move into it, your holy vision awakens.

As angels aren't limited by time and space, you can say the following prayer anywhere you want. If you feel that you'd like to boost this process, it's always good to go somewhere that feels particularly aligned with spirit. Maybe you have an altar or you can go to your favourite temple and quietly recite the prayer to yourself. Wherever works for you works for heaven.

✧   Sit down quietly and allow your eyes to close.

✧   Just breathe.

✧ Imagine a light of pure indigo washing over your whole body and especially around your forehead.

✧ Feel yourself being massaged and supported by this light.

✧ See between your brows a third eye opening. It's blinking a little, but shining with divine light.

✧ Visualize that eye bright with splendour and clearly able to see. Know you are in touch with your holy vision.

✧ Say this prayer:

'Thank you, spirits of place and angels of holy vision, for drawing close to me and bringing with you a true sense of connection to holiness.

I allow my third eye centre to release all resistance to forgiveness in my perception and vision so I can see the light as it is.

I now accept the balancing energy of spirit and the angels and allow it to move into my third eye centre, the point in my body that has to do with how I perceive the world and spirit.

I am grateful to be in touch with my inner vision and I allow it to align with love now and forevermore.

And so it is!'

The Crown Chakra: *Sahasrara*

Sahasrara is a Sanskrit word that means 'thousandfold' and this chakra is found at the crown of the head. Mystics over time have described it as a thousand-petalled lotus flower that opens at the tip of the crown and reaches up to several inches above the head. It is the energy centre that has to do with our connection to God/source/the divine and it is seen as a beautiful violet-white light.

This energy of this centre affects and is affected by:

- our spiritual growth
- our connection to God
- how we see the divine

If our crown chakra were in nature, it would be the life-force that connects every cell and atom. It is the energy that moves through every living being; it is the sky, the ground, the air, sun, and the seed – it is everything. It is God.

When the energy of the crown chakra gets blocked, it can cause a real sense of loneliness because this is our spiritual connection to our Creator. If we lose faith in God, or even ourselves, the thousand-petalled lotus can close, just as a lotus will close when the sun goes down.

When the crown chakra closes, we feel disconnected from the world. We're faced with challenges and blame a higher source rather than take responsibility for ourselves. However, in my eyes, the crown chakra never *fully* closes. Even in the darkest of times, there's still a crack of light from the universe waiting to hold and support us.

I also like to say that even if someone's completely atheist, that doesn't mean they can't have a balanced crown chakra. Sometimes there will be heaps of joy and light in the firmest of non-believers. That's a sure sign they're still following their chosen pathway.

Forgiveness through the crown chakra helps us to come to a positive space with God. In particular, if we've had challenging experiences with the idea of God, or even the word 'God', forgiveness is required. 'God' is not a religious word – people make God religious. God is the energy of creation, the macrocosm and the microcosm, the energy in everything that is, has been and will be. God is the universe and the universe is God.

The energy of the crown chakra calls us to release the limitations other people have imposed on us through the idea of God. For example, if we were brought up in a fundamentally religious home and were forced to fear the source of creation, forgiveness is needed. Recognizing that God is an energy of love and acceptance is the most important acknowledgement we can ever make, because it helps us to know that we are loved and accepted.

As we move into greater spiritual awareness, the crown chakra opens more and more. It's the chakra that is linked to our growth and our ability to stay spiritually aware even when we're faced with challenges. It's the centre that I would say has to do with our acceptance of whatever happens to us in life. It helps us to move forward, with love and forgiveness, from that space of acceptance.

Forgiveness and the Crown Chakra

Before opening this centre and bringing it into alignment with the six other chakras you've worked on, it's important to ensure that you're aware of any limitations you've created for yourself through resistance to forgiveness in the crown centre. Take a look at:

How You View God
Have you been frustrated by God? Do you feel that God is to blame for the experiences you've endured?

It's important to know that God doesn't choose that you should be hurt or go through challenges. God is complete acceptance and love

– and wants you to feel accepted and loved. You were given free will at your creation, as was everyone else, and you are given it now. Are you ready to see that God is love and in so doing forgive yourself for thinking that He wanted to punish you? In His eyes of course, you are always forgiven.

How Spiritual You Think You Are

This is a fundamental idea to work on through forgiveness and the crown chakra. Many people, when they move into spirituality, allow themselves to think that they're more connected to the divine than others, when really that isn't the truth at all. There's no course, label, certificate or attunement that's going to make you *more* connected to the divine or *more* spiritual. You're already connected and you're already spirit – the only thing that needs to change is your awareness. Knowing that *everyone* is equal and *everyone* is spirit helps you to move into a state of forgiveness, aware that love is within us all. It also allows you to release any élitist grievances your ego may be holding on to.

Connect with Source

Now that you've worked through any areas that require your forgiveness within the crown chakra, you have the chance to align all seven wheels of forgiveness and move forwards in a more loving, accepting way. God and His holy angels will manifest themselves through the thousand-petalled lotus chakra in order for you to feel more connected to everything that has been, is and ever will be.

Do this meditation anywhere that feels safe and comfortable to you:

✦ Visualize a piercing white light coming down from the sky and kissing the top of your head.

✦ With that kiss, a beautiful lotus flower opens at your crown. It shines out bright and beautiful.

✧ Take some time to recognize that God, the angels and all of the ancestor spirits who went before you are close to you now.

Here's a prayer:

'Thank you, Heavenly Father, Universal Source of Creation, for igniting in me the sparks of divinity that I may have forgotten about. I welcome you and your angels now to remove all thoughts that stand between me and my connection with you.

I now release all ideas of fear and punishment, knowing truly that your essence is nothing but love and acceptance.

I now accept the balancing energy of source and allow it to move into my crown chakra, which opens like a beautiful lotus with 1,000 petals.

I allow my chakras to come into a perfect alignment, creating a sense of heaven on Earth.

I forgive myself and every living being and every soul that has touched my life. I forgive and I am forgiven.

And so it is!'

Chapter 9
THE MIND IS AN ALTAR

'The Journey to God is merely the reawakening of the knowledge of where you are always, and what you are forever.'
A COURSE IN MIRACLES

I've been fascinated by altars for years. In fact, there's one in nearly every room of my home and I have three in my office space. I just love creating sacred spaces where I can honour the divine.

When I think back to how I discovered altars, the first memory that pops into my head is of when I was around three or four. A neighbour called Margaret would come to look after me then, especially when my parents were attending to my unwell nana. She would always make me my favourite meals and let me choose a sweet from her tub of wee assorted chocolates. Basically, she'd spoil me as if I was part of her own family.

I remember one afternoon she was looking after me because my parents were with my nana in hospital and I went along with her and her husband, Jim, to Mass. Margaret and Jim were brilliant family-orientated folk – in fact, they still are. They are devout Catholics and have always lived an honest life. Their son even went on to become a priest.

On this particular afternoon after Mass, I remember Margaret taking me down to the front of the church, where there was a shrine with a statue of a pale woman whose arms were by her side with her palms facing forwards. She was covered in a blue shawl and in front of her were red votives with candles inside.

'Who's that?' I asked, pointing towards the statue.

Margaret smiled, saying, 'It's Our Lady, my boy. She's the mother of wee baby Jesus.'

I knew the name 'Jesus', but I didn't fully understand his purpose at this point, so I just went, 'Oh. And what are we doing here?'

Margaret smiled again. 'I'm going to light a wee candle for your nana and pray to God for her. I'm going to pray that he helps her to feel better. You know, because she's not been feeling herself.'

I did know that my nana didn't have rosy red cheeks anymore and that she'd spent a lot of time in her wheelchair lately. I really hoped that what we were doing would help.

This was my first experience of lighting candles and connecting with altars, and I've been obsessed ever since. Just the other night, while I was writing this book, my friend John came to visit me for a few beers and a catch-up. He went to leave his jacket in my bedroom and came out saying, 'Man, it's like a statue shop in there – there are candles and gods everywhere! Not to mention it smells like a church!'

He had a point. Right now I have an altar by my bed with a huge brass Ganesh, the elephant god, from India. Beside him is a large citrine crystal (for abundance), a Virgin Mary candle from Mexico and a red candle for Mary Magdalene, plus prayer beads and other things. Then on my other chest of drawers I have photographs of the Dalai Lama and statues of the Tibetan goddess Green Tara, the Indian god Shiva, the monkey god Hanuman and another Ganesh. As you can probably tell, I'm a bit mixed up! I love all religious and spiritual iconography and it doesn't matter where it comes from! For me, all of these beings and gods actually come from the same place and they will all lead us back to love.

I read many years ago in a book by Diana Cooper that if we have only spiritual books and objects in our space, we'll raise its vibration and keep it connected to the divine. Ever since then I've kept spiritual items and books in my room – if I make the place somewhere the divine would like to spend time, then it's good enough for me.

Our Mind

Our mind is a powerful place. Everything we do and choose and focus on in our life is processed through it. There's no great way to describe it, though, because we've never actually seen it. In fact, we don't even know where it is. Most of us think it's in our head, but the facts tell us that's where our *brain* is. So, where is the mind?

For me, the mind is our essence. It's an inner translator that's suspended between love and fear – and we get to choose which of those voices to listen to. It's like in the old *Tom and Jerry* cartoons where you see an angel on one shoulder and a devil on the other – that's exactly what we face daily.

The devil on our shoulder is actually our ego. It's the voice of fear, the voice that wants to challenge our beliefs and our sense of worth. Its job is to challenge us – to question our capacity to accept love. We can spend a lot of the time spellbound by the ego and its false promises.

The angel on our other shoulder is our soul voice, our inner teacher or what *A Course in Miracles* calls 'the Holy Spirit'. It's the love and acceptance that can be forgotten when we decide to follow the voice of fear. But the inner teacher is the part of us that will lead us directly to our angels and our Creator.

I like to imagine the mind like an altar. It's in the centre of a beautiful holy temple and whatever is laid upon it is handed directly to the divine. It's the sacred space within our being that stands in front of God's throne, the space where we recognize that we're never separate, we're part of everything that is, was and ever will be.

As *A Course in Miracles* says, 'There is no time, no place, no state where God is absent. There is nothing to be feared.'

Take some time to really acknowledge that this powerful space within us is important for our journey through forgiveness. Right there, naked on that altar, is our real self. In that space, in our mind, is where all our ideas of forgiveness, love and acceptance are formed. It's good to know this space and to acknowledge the impact it can have.

The Divine Is Within

I've written and spoken about spirituality for years. I'm always teaching people that they have a beautiful connection to the divine within and their angels are always close by. It isn't anything new to me, but one day something was different.

I'd been listening to some brilliant tunes as I'd been driving to my office. I'd probably been driving too fast as well, because I got there quicker than I'd anticipated.

I love my office space so much and in particular I love my altars. Every day I go in and light candles and incense, and acknowledge the holy figures that represent God in my life.

Often I do my *Course in Miracles* practice when I get to the office. That particular day I was meeting my friend Hollie on Skype about 30 minutes after I got in, so I thought I'd light some candles and do my daily lesson right away. I lit the candles in my main room and then went back into the room with my desk to grab the *Course*. I usually write down a few things in my journal as I scan through the lesson and then I meditate on the affirmations or its core message when I've finished.

That day it was Lesson 157. I remember reading out loud, 'Into His presence would I enter now,' and really trying to get my head around it. It was talking about entering into the presence of God, the presence of our own holiness and the presence of Christ consciousness. It was big!

In a trance I felt myself stand up and walk through to my main room. In front of my Divine Mother altar I fell to my knees, then I said out loud again, 'Into His presence would I enter now,' and I began to cry. I was crying so hard that my mouth opened wide and I could feel snot, tears and who knows what else dripping down my face, but I was releasing pain and experiencing what I can only describe as pure joy.

It had occurred to me at that moment that I was one with the divine. I was literally connected to God.

Normally I do know this, but I'm so busy trying to keep up with my schedule and do everything else I need to do that I easily forget.

Not only that, but when I took that moment to acknowledge God and to move into His presence, I wasn't moving away from myself but moving back *within*.

I sat there sobbing for what felt like two minutes but was more like 30. Eventually, I could hear my Skype ringing in the next room. I grabbed tissues, tried to clean myself up and went to answer the call.

Hollie Holden is one of the most beautiful people I know. She gets me. She and her husband, Robert, are some of my best friends in the world. They are so real and we can speak about the goofiest of things or have deep heartfelt conversations about the divine. Hollie and Robert have not only become great friends to me but also mentors, especially with the *Course*, so this call felt like divine synchronicity.

Hollie quickly realized that I was crying and said, 'Oh, babe, are you OK?'

With real effort, I managed to tell her what had just happened. Well, I got as far as saying, 'And it just occurred to me, His presence is in me and I'm in Him and we're together,' before starting to weep again.

'And how are we even *supposed* to cope with that?' Holly replied.

I started to laugh. She was right, though – this was *big* stuff. The recognition that we are love and are connected to it eternally – what's bigger than that?

To understand this, picture a holy temple. Inside this temple there's a beautiful altar filled with spiritual items, candles and shiny things. In front of it is a pure divine light, the Holy Spirit, and all it does is love and accept.

You might like to meditate on the following:

You are the holy temple.

Your mind is an altar to the divine.

Within your temple is a bright light.

The bright light is accepting and loving.

Daily you stand before God.

Recognize him and recognize your Holiness.

You are never separate from Love.

According to *A Course in Miracles*:

You cannot understand how much your Father loves you, for there is no parallel in your experience of the world to help you understand it. There is nothing on Earth with which it can compare, and nothing you have ever felt apart from it resembles it ever so faintly.

Dressing the Altar

Now that we've recognized that we have within us an altar placed before the divine, it's important to see what we're putting on it.

The short answer to this is: everything that's in our head. Every single thought we have is displayed to the divine. Our angels, Creator and loved ones in heaven see every one, so it's important to align our thoughts with where we want to be.

I like to describe thoughts as magnetic. Every single thought we have pulls an experience or situation towards it. The state of our mind will determine the type of experience. What are you drawing towards you now – challenges or miracles?

It seems crazy that what we choose to have in our mind determines the miracles we have in our life. But every thought we think creates what happens next in our life. And aren't we entitled to miracles? That's why it's important to have our miraculous mindset on. When we choose to be just like our angels and like our Creator and to move forwards in a loving, forgiving and accepting way, we draw experiences that are loving and accepting and we are forgiven by those we feel are holding a grudge.

Even when something challenges us, we can decide how to react. It may not be easy, but remember one thing: *breathe.*

I believe that when we take some time to listen to our inner voice and look at our thoughts, it's as if we're giving the altar a dust. We're picking up the beautiful items and we're giving them a right good clean. Not only that, but if there are things that have managed to get on the altar that aren't serving us anymore or aren't supposed to be there, we can take them off and replace them with something new.

Clearing the Altar of Your Mind

Recently while on a trip to the United States I had the beautiful opportunity to go and stay with my friend Kate Northup and her new husband, Mike, in Portland, Maine. I was really excited to hang out with both of these guys because we'd hit it off the day we met, which was when Kate and I were speaking at an 'I Can Do It' conference in Hamburg, Germany.

While I was visiting Kate and Mike, we got to do so many lovely things, like go to yoga classes and the gym and have dinner on the harbourside. Maine is a beautiful place and my stay there really felt 'the way life should be', as it says on the welcome sign when you arrive.

Staying with these guys was a huge eye-opener for me and I can only consider it healing. If you don't know about Kate already, you need to check her out. She wrote an amazing book called *Money, a Love Story* that is doing special work helping to heal people and their fears around finances.

I didn't think I had any fears around finances. Fear to me is basically unforgiven thoughts about a subject and for a 26-year-old I was doing pretty well. When it came to my business, I'd always made more than enough to pay for my rent, car and whatever else, but to be truthful I was still living at home and definitely preventing opportunities for abundance coming my way.

Kate is a loving, sensitive soul and she doesn't force any of her ideas down your throat. She didn't tell me to change anything about my life, but her demonstration of her spiritual practice and how it connected to finances really struck me.

Kate loves speaking about business, not because she's greedy or she wants to have more than anyone else, but because deep down she knows it will demonstrate to others that it's possible to create a happy, abundant and joyous lifestyle. So every day we'd end up speaking about something related to business and I began to notice what I was doing when it happened – I was flinching. My body was physically reacting to what I felt deep inside. I had to check out what was going on.

Truth be told, I felt overworked and I was definitely underpaid. I realized that I'd spent my whole life as a young adult in the service of others, and while I'd been doing that, my own life had been put on hold. Not only that, but I'd felt it was my duty to make my services more than affordable so I could help every single person I could, but at the same time I'd been sacrificing creating a home for myself by refusing to let my career grow naturally. I had to admit it to myself: I was scared, I was tired and I was overcome with financial fear.

Although I didn't tell Kate or Mike what was going on, I'm more than certain these beautifully intuitive and intelligent people knew anyway. I do remember telling them about my waiting list – that it had over 900 people on it and I was trying to get through each and every person but I hadn't changed my rates in years and they weren't reflecting my reputation. I also told them that I was desperate to do an online course and get my teaching to the masses so that I could help more than one person at a time.

Over the five-day trip, Kate gently encouraged me to see that I was getting in the way of abundance. In fact, I was putting 'lack' right up there on the altar of my mind.

Changing Thoughts

On my second-to-last night we'd arranged to take a trip to a place called Portsmouth, an hour and a half away, to meet up with our dear friend Cheryl Richardson and her husband, Michael. We went to an amazing French restaurant and it was just so lovely to be around like-minded people. We all spoke about our recent adventures and I shared what I was doing and how I was writing a book on forgiveness. It really was fantastic. Of course, as I was sitting with a money expert and a self-care expert at the one table, it was only a matter of time before the subject turned to abundance.

During our conversation I spoke about my concerns in business and how I was finding it extremely difficult to increase my prices while still staying loyal to my local followers. I opened up honestly about how my amazing mum and I had been able to pay off all our debts and get in a really positive space with our finances, but how I'd also realized that I was stopping myself from growing.

Cheryl told me that I was entitled to abundance and the universe was desperate to support me. She assured me that life would love to step in, but I needed to get out of the way first. In that moment all of my limiting thoughts started rushing through my mind – and then it came to me that I needed to stop being so darn stubborn and allow myself to grow. I realized that comparing my earnings to those of my friends from school wasn't healthy for me or them. I needed to drop comparison and to stop basing my success on my earnings – I needed to forgive myself for my financial mindset and let it go.

I was feeling inspired. It was amazing to be around people who could hear me for who I was and understand where I was standing. Cheryl then pulled out her Grace cards and encouraged me to pick one. I said out loud, 'Thank you, angels, for revealing to me what I need to know,' and then chose one.

The card read: 'Receive: When we open ourselves up to others, we open ourselves up to the abundance of the universe.'

I burst into tears. Right there in the middle of the restaurant, I started to do the ugly cry.

The waitress turned up with the sweet menu, took one look and said, 'Oh, sorry, I'll come back in a moment!'

'Don't worry,' I said quickly, 'we're all therapists!'

Everyone laughed.

Kate, Cheryl, Mike and Michael all helped me to see that what I was laying down on the altar of my mind was blocking my ability to receive. They explained that I could change it and I could do it right there. Cheryl said, 'Ask God to give you more money so you can share it with others if that will make you feel better.'

I started to type a prayer into my phone:

'Thank you, God, for giving me more money to nourish myself and to share with others.

And so it is!'

And healing occurred in that moment. I shifted my thoughts from lack to plenty and from fear to love. I realized that God was more than happy to supply abundance if I could just allow it to happen. I forgave myself for my past choices and I felt forgiven.

On the way home in the car that night, Kate, Mike and I discussed how powerful dinner had been, and even though a part of me felt exposed, I felt completely accepted. We discussed ways of changing how I was doing things and how I could get my teaching out to the world. I made a list of some things I could do and with Kate's support I managed to put them in order of priority.

I set myself a goal of making £10,000 in a month so I could put away money for a deposit on a home of my own and I kept using my prayer and forgiveness mindset. I created an online course and it sold out in seven days. I had exceeded my £10k already – it was miraculous.

Leaving Maine felt emotional. I can't wait to go back and create more miracles with my adopted sister Kate and her family.

My trip showed me clearly what I was placing on the altar of my mind. What are you laying on yours? Is it serving you?

Create an Altar

Having an altar is a wonderful way to have a physical representation of what you're holding in your mind. As I said earlier, whatever you think about most, you're pretty much contributing towards creating. Are you creating forgiveness? There are loads of books out there on the Law of Attraction and manifesting what you want, and it's exactly the same when it comes to forgiveness. When you think forgiving thoughts, you draw forgiving situations and people to you, and when you think the opposite, well, you can imagine what you begin to face.

When you think forgiving thoughts it's as if the altar of your mind is given candles. They are lit and they burn so gently, contributing towards peace. This peace not only resides within your holy temple but extends out like a wave, touching all those you meet on your path.

As you now know, I've a great love for altars, so I have many of them. I treat them as physical spaces that help me to cultivate my thoughts and the energy I'm giving off to others.

An example is the Ganesh altar I have in my bedroom. Ganesh is the remover of obstacles. Indian teachings tell us he gets rid of whatever stands between us and inner peace. I love that whole idea, so I created a space in my room where I could go daily and hold the intention that I was free of any obstacle that stood between me and peace.

My Ganesh altar has a citrine crystal on it because crystal therapy teaches us that citrine is a stone that contributes to abundance. I put it there to remind me that abundance goes beyond finances; it's also about recognizing the blessings we already have.

I've also got *mala* prayer beads that a friend, Natalia, made for me, with a gold Mary Magdalene charm on. I absolutely love them. They help me to remember that this ascended master is able to encourage me to move back into the cave of my heart at any time and from that space the miracle of forgiveness is possible.

I also have a Virgin Mary candle my friend Anna brought me back from Texas. I have a deep affinity with the Divine Mother and I know she's never far from me when I need her loving guidance and acceptance.

Now that you're at the stage of moving into the miracle of forgiveness and remembering your loving connections, why not prepare a space in your home that can be the physical representation of the positive work you are doing within? Clear a part of your bookshelf, bedside table or even mantelpiece. Fill it with items that make you remember love and help you to stay focused on creating a miracle mindset.

Remember that a miracle mindset is accepting, trusting and loving. It's the perfect space within that remembers your wholeness and it's the part of you that will never allow you to be a victim of your worst nightmare. It's the *real* you that is never separate from the divine.

To help you to reflect on this, here's a closing meditation prayer:

> 'There is an altar in the centre of my mind,
>
> a place so holy, where angels dwell.
>
> In this space is a perfect me: loving, accepting and whole.
>
> I now enter the holy temple and kneel before this altar.
>
> I welcome the ever-present love that awaits.
>
> I release all resistance and return to meet my Creator.
>
> Thank you, God, for entering the space in my mind where you already abide.
>
> Thank you, God, for sending your angels to stand around my being.
>
> I am protected by holy light. Archangels and holy ones guard me here.
>
> It's so good to be here with you again. It's so good to be accepted.
>
> And so it is.'

Chapter 10
INTO THE LIGHT

*'He does not know shadows. His eyes look
past error to the Christ in you.'*
THE SONG OF PRAYER, *A COURSE IN MIRACLES*

My journey into the wings of forgiveness has been interesting. It's been the first time while writing a book that I've felt the need to go to sacred sites to download information and gain insight.

To be honest, I thought it was going to be easier than it has been. Writing my last three books felt a lot simpler. They were all on angels, and angels are my life, so it was second nature to share what I knew. Forgiveness is different – it's a lesson I've learned and will never stop learning. It's been a great reminder that I'm a student on this pathway, not a teacher.

I honestly believed when I signed the contract for this book that the universe had another idea. I felt that I was signing a spiritual agreement to fully understand and embody what it meant to forgive and be forgiven.

When I learned that Mary Magdalene was my guide to forgiveness and that her angels were bringing through support for this planet, I decided to look into places that may have been connected to Mary. I turned to *The Da Vinci Code* for inspiration. It may be fiction, but I had the feeling that even if it wasn't 100 per cent correct, so many people believed the story that it could have conjured up Magdalene energy that I could connect to.

I was trying to find a physical space to complement the emotions and experiences that I was going through on an inner level. The first one that came to mind was Rosslyn Chapel, near Edinburgh.

Searching

I woke up early one Sunday morning. It had been many years since I'd visited Rosslyn and I was excited. I packed my bag with a few things that had been helping me on my journey: a postcard print of Mary Magdalene by a talented artist called Lily Moses and a Scarlet Temple quartz crystal that I'd been meditating with.

I'd only learned about Scarlet Temple quartz when I started out on this adventure. Crystals have always had a huge influence on my spiritual practice, though, because crystal healing was the first healing system I ever studied.

My friend Liam Wood is a well-known and respected crystal supplier. He always posts the rarest and most beautiful crystals on his page. In fact, I have his website listed as one of my favourites, because I'm always checking to see what wonderful and shiny things he has in.

Randomly one day I checked his page and saw a listing for Scarlet Temple quartz. It was a palm-sized naturally pointed quartz crystal, but it had a deep red running through the centre, I think from iron in the mineral.

I was excited because 'Scarlet Temple' had Goddess/ Magdalene energy written all over it. I looked around online and found that people believed Scarlet Temple quartz was used by priestesses in the ancient land of Lemuria to gain blessings from the Goddess, and that was good enough for me.

So off I went with my crystal, the Mary Magdalene picture and my journal to Rosslyn Chapel.

As soon as I arrived I felt inspired, but to be terribly honest with you, I wasn't getting the hit I wanted. I looked around the beautiful chapel with its starry roof and gorgeous stained-glass windows. I joined the tour and listened to the history of the chapel and how the stonemasons had created it. But there was no mention of Mary Magdalene.

I went outside. I walked round the chapel and found a quiet little spot looking out onto the beautiful hills beyond the chapel. I sat down, held my crystal and gazed at my picture of Mary Magdalene.

'Where are you?' I whispered. 'I want to learn more.'

Closing my eyes, I breathed quietly and listened within. I felt a sense of calm, but there were no dramatic events, no angels and no messages from Mary Magdalene. I was a little bit disappointed to say the least, but that's what happens from time to time.

I went back into the chapel for a while to light a candle for Meggan Watterson, who had unconsciously reawakened my love for Mary Magdalene and helped me to connect to her, as I explained earlier. I wrote, 'For Meggan Watterson and her sacred work with women,' in the book and headed off home.

Weeks went by and I realized I probably had enough information to fill my book on forgiveness, but I also had a burning desire to go to Glastonbury. I had the feeling that it would provide the perfect space for me to open up to heaven.

Adventure Calling

One night I was telling my good friend Sara about this project. She seemed really interested and it's always good to share what you're working on with like-minded friends.

I'd met Sara a few years earlier when I'd been speaking in Stratford-upon-Avon. She lives in Coventry and we always keep in touch via Facebook. Sara also loves everything to do with angels, crystals and spirituality, so we're always liking and sharing each other's posts.

Sara had just been to Avebury, but she hadn't had as strong a spiritual connection there as she'd hoped, and there was I sharing the exact same outcome from my trip to Rosslyn. I told her I felt really drawn to Glastonbury and I didn't know why. She'd been there before, but only for a flying two-hour visit. It seemed perfect. I asked her if she wanted to join me on an adventure exploring the sacred sites of Glastonbury and two weeks later our journey began.

We met in the hotel car park with hugs and giggles. It had been a whole year or so since we'd seen each other, so we had a bit of a catch-up before jumping into my hire car and going off into the centre of Avalon!

Glastonbury is an overwhelming place, but overwhelming in the most beautiful way. The energy is high; at first I felt a little sick and my head was pounding, but it didn't feel negative. I knew I was experiencing some sort of shift, but I was yet to find out about that.

In the past when I'd heard people talking about Glastonbury, I'd always been a little sceptical because they'd always say the most wonderful things about it and it couldn't be that good, surely? But I was wrong – it really is magical. Every corner you turn there's something exciting happening and the High Street is just full of shops selling everything crystal, spiritual, magical, healing and angel-related – with a huge Goddess emphasis.

Sara and I strolled around the shops while filling each other in on all the recent happenings in our lives. We went to every store we felt drawn to and looked at all the crystals and

Goddess figures. But although there were some lovely things there, nothing was jumping out at me.

It all changed when we went to a store called Stone Age. Every spiritual friend on my Facebook had told me about it. Stone Age is down a little lane filled with crystals. They're embedded in the walls and there's loads of amazing imagery outside too, including a huge Buddha.

The door of the store was locked, but there was a sign on it that read, 'Back in 10 minutes,' so we stayed there and peered in the window. The place glistened. Crystals everywhere were shining in the light. Then something caught my eye. There in the centre of the main cabinet in the window was a Black Madonna statue made of obsidian, about 30cm tall. The display was on one of those motors that rotate items 360° and I must have watched the Madonna spin at least 30 times, because all of a sudden the store was open for business and we were inside.

I felt almost as though I was in a trance. I looked around the store, but I couldn't take my mind off the Black Madonna. She was haunting my thoughts, but I knew she was going to cost more than my flights and hotel put together. I had to ask how much she was.

The lovely lady behind the desk, dressed in a purple flowing top, walked over with the keys to open the cabinet. She took out the statue and told me, 'She's £395.'

I just replied, 'Thank you,' and we got ready to go.

But when we tried to leave, I just couldn't get out of the door. It was as though a massive big angel was standing there saying, 'Do not pass.' I was missing something.

I was in Glastonbury – everyone there is pretty spiritually aware – so I said, 'I really feel drawn to the Black Madonna. It's as though I can't leave without her, but she's a little above budget!'

The lady then shouted, 'Lui, can you give a better deal for the Black Madonna in the cabinet?'

A voice from upstairs replied, 'How much is it?'

'It's 395 quid.'

I could hear someone coming downstairs. Then a man was smiling at me, saying, 'Is it you who wants the Black Madonna? She's very powerful.'

'I know – I'm very drawn to her!' I said, smiling back.

'I'll give you £100 off,' he said.

'Sold.'

Five minutes later I was walking out of the store with a considerably heavier backpack.

Chalice Well

After a rest back at the hotel we were ready to go back into Glastonbury. We planned to visit the Chalice Well. I knew that this was going to be an interesting trip because the *vesica piscis* symbol that I'd seen in my lucid dream with Mary Magdalene and the Myriam was the same shape as the pool at the bottom of the well gardens.

I wrapped my Black Madonna in a towel and took some crystals with me to be cleansed and blessed by the water at the well. There was no hiding it – I was so excited! I went down and knocked on Sara's door and she answered it jumping for joy and excitement, too! I was so glad that someone as mad as me was on this trip with me, and what was even funnier was that Sara had two bags with her and one of those was filled with crystals that she wanted to cleanse at the well.

We arrived at the Chalice Well Gardens entrance and purchased our tickets. The lovely lady there gave us a map and bottles in which to capture some of the well water to take home with us and off we went.

As soon as we walked into the gardens there was a definite change of energy – complete serenity washed over both of us. It was as though a gentle silence was kissing our heads.

Sara wanted to visit the bathroom before we went exploring, so I decided to sit on the bench next to the *vesica piscis* pool and wait for her. I closed my eyes and breathed deeply and I could sense my entire being opening up.

I was continuing to follow my breath when all of a sudden a light wind tickled the back of my neck, raising every hair. I opened my eyes and there, standing next to the fountains at the *vesica piscis* pool, was one of the Myriam angels. It was so bright and light and looked so otherworldly, it was indescribably beautiful. Tears filled my eyes. After a few seconds the angel just vanished, but I knew it was close by.

I looked over my shoulder and saw Sara was on her way back, but I couldn't even tell you how long she'd taken. I got up and went over to her. 'They're here,' I said with a smile and we began to walk deeper into the well gardens.

As you enter what I would consider the main part of the complex, just before the healing pools, there are two huge yew trees. It's as if they are nature's guardian spirits, ensuring that only those with love in their heart enter this healing sanctuary. I couldn't help but want to give the trees a massive big hug – they felt so warm.

As we walked towards the healing pools we could see a bunch of children with their feet in the water playing with their mother. It was lovely to see.

We kept walking past and like magnets we could feel ourselves being drawn to the lion's head fountain. As soon as we were there, I knew I had to drink from the healing waters.

When we'd entered the gardens, the lovely lady who'd welcomed us in had mentioned that the water had a high iron content and that it might take us a few sips to get used to it. With that in mind, I took my little bottle and began to fill it. I then held it up, peered in for a second and took my first sip…

'It tastes, it tastes, it tastes like…' Looking up, I tried to think.

'Blood,' Sara replied.

She was right. The water tasted like blood. It felt so holy and auspicious to me. Could it represent the blood of Mother Earth or even the blood of Christ? I just knew that whatever was happening here today was some sort of initiation or process through which I was completing my journey of forgiveness. I felt a sense of restoration as I drank my 'ironized' water from the well.

Sara and I both went into a short silence as we took our crystals and washed them under the well. Sara laid hers out in a grid format while I sat in quiet meditation, waiting to cleanse my new Black Madonna statue.

I remember feeling the cold water trickling down my arms as I held her under the water. I was baptizing my new icon in water that tasted like blood. She was being blessed by the blood of Mother Earth while being washed with water like Christ – it was mesmerizing. My heart felt as though it was going to burst with love.

I then took a towel out of my bag and allowed the statue to sit on it as the cool air of the summer afternoon dried her.

As we sat there enjoying the atmosphere, a lovely Asian lady came to fill her bottle from the fountain. She was wearing an old-fashioned gardening hat and white clothes. Around her neck was a bright red pashmina.

I shuffled to the side with my Black Madonna. 'Sorry – I'll move out the way for you.'

'No problem. What's that you have there?' she said, pointing directly at my statue.

I held up the Black Madonna so she could see her.

'It's a Black Madonna statue. I got her here in Glastonbury and I've just blessed her with water from the well.'

'Madonna, you say? My name is the Indian name for Madonna or Divine Mother: I'm Shakti.'

'How lovely to meet you! You've no idea how important it was to hear that!'

The lady smiled and walked out of the garden.

'What's going on?' I asked Sara. 'I just feel that the divine is here with us right now – I mean, they couldn't send any more signs to confirm they're on this trip with us!'

All of a sudden peaceful music started to play. It was a saxophone and it was some of the most beautiful sounds I've ever heard. It was as if the musician was playing a sultry love song to his partner, but I felt that the divine was playing a love song to me.

'Is it just me? Is that music in my head or is it real?'

Sara began to laugh. 'No, silly, it's not in your head! It's as though the angels are playing to us.'

I could see she, too, was quite struck by the energy and events of the day.

Time had slipped away. We could feel it was getting later and I knew the gardens closed at six, so we packed our things and continued walking towards the top of the well.

Mother and Child

There's a beautiful opening at one point in the gardens, almost like a little outdoor chapel, where there's a stone carving of a mother and child with candles all around. Two benches are provided there for people to sit on and meditate peacefully. I walked in, saw the statue and my clairvoyance instantly kicked in. I felt that the mother was Mary Magdalene and the child was me. I felt Mary's loving arms wrap around me as I was consumed by a red light of unconditional love. I fell to my knees and was embraced by the unseen presence, but inside my mind I could see myself being held by the Beloved.

After a few minutes I managed to bring myself back to Earth, pulled a tea light from my bag and lit it on the altar hosting the mother and child. I took a few silent moments to be grateful and my nana came to my mind. Without her visit at the time of her physical passing when I was only four years old, I knew I wouldn't have been in the position I was in now. I was grateful. I was blessed.

I didn't even know where Sara was, but that didn't matter. I knew she'd be experiencing her own connections.

I stood up, still looking at the mother and child, and then I suddenly saw the Myriam angels in front of me. I gasped, as their presence was so unexpected. They drew closer and closer until they were right in front of me. I was eye to eye with these angels – the angels who awaken our holy vision, the angels who bring us back from grief and ultimately the angels who help us to understand forgiveness.

I had the overwhelming sensation that the Myriam were asking me if I was ready to fully understand and live within the wings of forgiveness – the wings that seemed to be attached to them. I felt my soul say a loud and clear: 'Yes!' Then the Myriam merged into one being and became a blade of light and with that they entered my heart.

Everything felt normal, but I seemed to be seeing the world around me in a new light. Could this be the awakening I was searching for?

Looking back, I think that when I was looking at the Myriam, I was looking at unconditional love, eye to eye, and was remembering what it was like to be completely held and completely forgiven.

It was an experience I'll never forget. I believe that when we really begin to open ourselves up to the miracle of forgiveness, the angels who guide the process will initiate us so we can truly represent it in the world.

Afterwards, Sara and I went to the wellhead and sat in meditation, just processing the energy we'd experienced that day. It was something else. I felt amazing. It was as if every barrier, block and fear from my body was being released. I felt that every exhale was expelling fear and every inhale was bringing in a deeper love.

Just before we left I asked Sara to take a picture of me at the wellhead. I peered inside and there, floating on top of the water, was a single white feather. Sure, the feather could have come from a bird, but for me it felt significant, as though it was a sign, a reminder that I was now walking within the wings of forgiveness.

Visions of the Black Madonna

Getting to bed that night was just what the doctor ordered. The whole day travelling from Glasgow to Bristol and then driving to Glastonbury had been intense enough without adding in yet more encounters with the angels of forgiveness and Mary Magdalene.

Sara and I had a chat over pizza in our pyjamas before bringing our night to a close. I headed for my room and got straight into bed. Lying there thinking, trying to process the day, I remembered my newly blessed Black Madonna statue. I jumped out of bed to go and get her from my bag. I unrolled her from the towel and put her on the bedside table, facing in my direction. I sat with my journal in my lap and wrote a prayer and blessing to reflect my experiences of the day. Here it is, word for word, dated 10 July 2014:

Beloved

I stand here now, stripped naked and prepared,
For I am ready to know forgiveness,
I am willing to share forgiveness,
And I am now living within the wings of forgiveness.

In complete humility I am exposed,
Sharing my realness with the world,
For I have now accepted the love that I am entitled to.

I am the child of humanity, an expression of light, the echo of
*   God's love.*
By remembering my true identity and accepting it now,
I draw choirs of angels close.
Holy angels and archangels surround me now.
They have prepared the way.
In complete trust I take their lead, for today I am honoured
*   and loved.*
I am the Beloved.

I sat there in my bed, filled with tears and a deep feeling of love. I felt prepared and as though forgiveness was moving though me – I think I got it. I gave myself five minutes of meditation then lay back, switched off the light and drifted into a deep sleep.

In the early hours of the morning I felt something wake me up. My eyes were so tired I could barely open them, but finally I managed to open up first my right eye and then my left. Floating above me was a red mist. What was stranger was that I felt uneasy with it.

From the mist, a dark female face emerged, peering into what I can only describe as my soul. At that moment, all I could do was surrender. I watched as the face consumed all the darkness from my body. It was as though she'd been sent to rip from my heart, body, mind and soul all the aspects that weren't complementing my journey of forgiveness.

It was strange, because a part of me felt scared and I don't know why. So I called out to one angel I knew wouldn't let me down: 'Thank you, Archangel Michael, for standing with me now and ensuring that I am safe.'

I remember feeling Michael and his angels coming close to me. I breathed with ease and drifted back into a deep sleep.

The next morning I slept through to nearly 10 a.m. Sara, on the other hand, had had a restful night and had woken at the crack of dawn, ready to face the day!

Exploring Deeper

We made our way back into Glastonbury for Day 2 of shopping and exploring the magnificent town. We'd heard that there was a raw chocolate shop at the top of the street we were on, so we decided to make our way up there. It was great feeling so connected to the energy of forgiveness and the ascended masters *and* being able to treat ourselves to goodies, including *healthy* chocolate!

While we were in the shop ordering Mulberry dark chocolate (which tasted incredible), we bumped into Sara's friend Ruth and her friend Phil. It was funny, because we'd just been speaking about Ruth. She is a lovely soul, who does loads for animals and is always sharing petitions to overcome animal cruelty and support campaigns to benefit the Earth. We all had a chat and I started to tell her about my adventure so far. She then said, 'Have you been to Magdalene Close yet?

There's a chapel down there called St Margaret's which has wonderful energy.'

I started to get excited. 'Oh my goodness! Can you take us?'

She smiled and nodded. Off we went.

We were all having a chat on our way down the High Street when I saw a man hand Sara a little piece of paper. She turned round to me, saying, 'This is incredible – you're not going to believe it!' and handed it to me.

It was a passage about Mary Magdalene and how she supposedly went to Glastonbury when she fled the Holy Land. There was no doubt about it – whether she went to Glastonbury back then or not, she was definitely with us *now*.

We arrived at St Margaret's Chapel and went inside to find it completely empty. There were just a few seats around the sides and a large empty space in the centre.

Ruth said, 'I've the feeling I want to make some sound to help us harness the energy that's moving with us today.'

She invited us all to stand in a circle holding hands and then, in a high-pitched, almost operatic voice, began to tone some amazing angelic sounds. There were no words, just sounds, but they spoke to my heart. Every hair on my body stood on end and I was overcome by the feeling that there were angels present. The sound grew and grew and all of a sudden I realized Ruth was channelling divine feminine energy to us. It was beautiful.

Eventually she stopped and we all sat down to ground ourselves. Then I noticed that there were candles and a donation box in the chapel. I went over to light a candle and realized there were two icons beside them. One was of St Margaret of Scotland and the other one was of my beloved Mary Magdalene. I said a silent prayer: 'Thank you, Mary Magdalene and the Myriam, for drawing close and revealing even more of yourselves to us!'

Ruth said, 'There's more sound ready to come through,' so we all quickly gathered in the centre of the empty chapel. Then she went off on one again, except this time the sounds were very deep and masculine. We all closed our eyes as she brought the divine voice healing to the space. But then I couldn't help it – I had to open my eyes. I wanted to see what was happening.

As I opened my eyes and looked at everyone else, I realized they were bathed in a pure white light like that of the Myriam. It then occurred to me that the voice coming through Ruth was divine masculine energy. It felt like Christ energy. We were being blessed by both the divine female and male.

Something caught my eye – a pure white butterfly. It came through the door and began to circle around us. As it was swooshing through the air above us, I recalled how in my book *Angel Prayers* I'd explained that a butterfly could be a message from heaven to say that someone was no longer in pain. It was a true sign of transformation. Now I felt that this butterfly was my higher self saying, '*Transformation.*' It was as though I was moving beyond the limitation of pain.

Facing Fear Full On

By this point, we'd been almost everywhere in Glastonbury, including the Tor. What an amazing hike that was and being able to stand underneath St Michael's Tower was absolutely exhilarating. There was only one place that we hadn't visited and I really don't know why we left it to last, but the angels did. It was called the White Spring.

I thought the spring would be a pure white stream running through greenery, but I thought wrong. To get to it, we walked up to just past the Chalice Well, then turned left and began walking up a little hill. About 300 metres up the hill was an old

Victorian building with a bunch of people outside, sitting on the ledges carved into its stonework.

A volunteer greeted us, saying, 'No phones, torches or pictures.' I looked into the well house and could barely see anything other than a few candles flickering in the air that was passing through. I remember instantly taking off my shoes and walking in with Sara on my left, while Ruth and her friend Phil went off and did their own thing.

Sara whispered to me, 'I'm actually a little bit scared in here. I'm not sure I feel comfortable with this amount of darkness in a place I don't know. I feel intimidated.'

'Really?' I replied. 'There's nothing to be afraid of here – there are angels everywhere!'

At first the place did seem pitch-black, but once my eyes adapted to the light I realized that in the centre of the well house were pools that young children were bathing in while their parents sat at the edge.

I felt myself doing that thing that's beginning to become natural when I visit sacred sites – I went into autopilot. I felt my body walking right over to the far left-hand corner of the room. Almost in a dream-like state I found myself before a Black Madonna statue that was bathed by candlelight. She was right before a little pool that had running water moving through it. I knew I had to get in – I had to be blessed by this healing water.

Sitting on the side of the healing pool, I rolled my shorts as high as they would go and plopped my feet into the freezing cold water. It came up to my thighs and was *so cold*, but I didn't care – I knew that healing was taking place.

I felt myself surrendering even more to the Black Madonna. I realized that she was the presence that had hovered over me in my bed the previous night and that even though there was darkness in this space now, in that blackness there was so much light.

The Black Madonna's energy swirled around me as I allowed her to remove the fears that stood between me and forgiveness. I realized then that she was an aspect of the Goddess and also an aspect of Mary Magdalene. I was being set free.

In my mind I could see the Myriam and angels of pure white light removing from my being the remainder of the darkness that no longer needed to be there. The Black Madonna was consuming all of my fear and releasing it. I was being washed clean. I was being baptized in holy healing light.

It occurred to me that darkness is something that many people fear because it hides the unknown and can be hard to control. But without darkness, light cannot shine.

The Black Madonna is an aspect of the divine that represents the unknown. She's a force that has an amazing ability to help us to see that our fears aren't as bad as we think — she's a reminder that we're all a channel of pure source energy.

The Black Madonna is within every man and every woman. She's that aspect of us that is deep, held in and emotional. She's the part of us that doesn't reveal to others what's going on within. She's the part that tells us to keep going even when our fear is almost too much for us to handle. She helps us to remember that light is available and we are the light that can shine through the darkness like a star in the night sky.

After being in the pools for a short time and releasing the energy that had caused me to feel fear, I had the feeling that there would be radical shifts happening in my life — changes would take place so that I could be a greater source of light. Not knowing what was going to happen felt daunting, but I trusted that what needed to happen would happen, because

I was standing within the wings of forgiveness and all these different faces of divine energy were here to remind me of that.

I went and sat outside with the rest of the guys in complete silence, allowing my soul, body and mind to adjust to whatever had just happened. I knew then that my exploration of forgiveness was just about done. Glastonbury had been such a source of light on this journey. I was ecstatic, emotional and lighter than I'd ever thought I could be.

Forgiveness Is Who I Am

After what can only be described as an eventful day, we thanked Ruth and Phil for their support on the adventure and headed back to the hotel for a rest.

While we were driving there, we realized it was a full moon and even though the sun was still up, the moon was up, too.

'Twilight,' I said, looking across at Sara as I drove.

I remember lying on top of my bed with my clothes and shoes on, trying to process what had happened that day. My mind just kept going back to all the synchronicities, reminders and visions that had happened during my visit. I mean, what are the odds of speaking about Mary Magdalene and then a random man in the street handing Sara a passage on her, or buying a Black Madonna, only to find there was one in the White Spring?

I felt that I'd truly come full circle with understanding forgiveness, overcoming the darkness within my life and embracing the light of my soul. But I also felt that there was something to come that would complete the process.

After a little nap and a shower, I decided it would make sense to walk back up the Tor one final time. It was full moon and a beautiful summer's night and I was going home tomorrow – I had to complete the trip in style.

I asked Sara and she said, 'I wanted to say the same thing – let's go!'

Walking up Glastonbury Tor is an exhilarating experience. It takes between 10 and 20 minutes, depending on how much energy you have. It's pretty steep, but I love a walk and it feels like a sacred pilgrimage as you walk up to St Michael's Tower at the top.

Sara and I walked at a different pace – I was slightly faster. It seemed that all the yoga sun salutations were paying off!

When we got to the top there were crowds of people gathering to watch the sun go down and the full moon come up. At one point, the moon was shining on our left and the sun on our right – they were in perfect alignment.

All the way through this book I hope you've recognized something that I find extremely important in spirituality: balance. I love following *A Course in Miracles*, but, as you've probably noticed, it's a predominantly 'he' text. I hope my fascination and connection with the divine 'she' has balanced it out for you. The sun in pagan spirituality always represents God, or divine masculine energy, whereas the moon represents the divine feminine. I felt in complete balance standing at the top of the Tor knowing that both the sun and the moon were shining on me and my life.

It was a mesmerizing experience up there and to complete it Sara and I gave thanks to the universe in the form of sun and moon, God and Goddess.

An Encounter with Forgiveness

Back at the hotel, we were looking through all the treasure we'd picked up on our journey and discussing how amazing it was to be there when I was interrupted by my phone flashing.

I picked it up and saw a message from my friend George. He told me that one of our mutual friends had mentioned me in a post and asked if I'd seen it.

I felt sick. Earlier on, the friend in question had randomly deleted and blocked me online. Our last message had been full of smiles and love hearts, but it seemed something had upset them. I decided to call George.

'Hi, man! What does it say?'

'Well, I'm sorry to be the one telling you this, Kyle. I didn't realize anything was wrong between you guys.'

'I didn't either.'

George told me that there were two drunken posts from the person I'd considered a close friend. They'd said different things, but included 'his book is a pile of shite' and that I deserved 'to rot in hell'.

I felt so betrayed. My mind started running all over the place. I remembered all the times I'd supported my so-called friend through the challenges in their life. Why were they doing this now? And what could I do about it? My ego kicked in and started to throw ideas into my mind. I was eye to eye with fear.

George was so supportive, but I knew he was feeling bad about being the one to tell me about the posts. And all the while Sara was sitting beside me, wondering what was going on.

After about 10 minutes of anger, frustration and fear, I checked myself. I was in the process of allowing someone else to make me believe I was phoney when I knew I was not, and I was letting someone else determine how I felt, when the truth was I had a choice about that.

I remembered the teachings of A Course in Miracles and knew that if I wanted to experience peace I had to remove any idea of 'attack' from my mind. I remembered my wholeness. I remembered my integrity. I told myself I didn't have to prove anything.

Right there I remembered that I could choose fear or I could choose love. I knew that forgiveness would return me to my natural state of love. So I had to forgive.

Sara sat in silence as I worked my way through it. Like a guardian angel, she supported me through my challenge but allowed me to make the choice about how I dealt with it.

I hit the floor in meditation position, crossed-legged with my palms facing upwards on my knees. I imagined myself surrounded by light and remembered the Myriam angels. I drew them close through visualization and knew they were there. I surrendered the grief this situation was causing me and remembered I was already whole and healed. I said out loud, 'Thank you for revealing to me more ways I can be forgiving!' and then I imagined love coming from my heart and reaching out to the person who had posted their thoughts about me all over the internet. And I felt free.

I knew I was never going to get to speak to that person, but in some way they were watching me. I posted a photo quote online that simply said, 'I love you and I forgive you,' and I felt huge relief.

I knew then that forgiveness had become a process for me. The Myriam penetrating my heart at the Chalice Well altar to the mother and child had done what was needed. I knew how to forgive. I was truly walking within the wings of forgiveness.

It was slightly surprising to go through that whole situation and release it within 30 minutes. To be honest, it was amazing! But there it was.

Sara and I had a chat and I thanked her for being there on the whole Glastonbury journey. She felt that I'd helped her, too. There was a true balance there. Our friendship had been strengthened by the encounters and events we'd experienced. She was leaving first thing, so we said our goodbyes and went to bed.

Glastonbury helped me know true forgiveness and for that I will be forever grateful.

Chapter 11
THE MASTERS OF FORGIVENESS

*'Miracles are natural signs of forgiveness. Through miracles
you accept God's forgiveness by extending it to others.'*
A COURSE IN MIRACLES

There is a congregation of powerful spiritual beings, angels, masters, gods and goddesses who are able to support us on our journey into the wings of forgiveness. We can call on them at any time – they aren't bound by time or space. They are here within the present moment, waiting for our call. These masters of forgiveness go beyond religion, even though some of them may have history with it. They are non-denominational spiritual leaders of unconditional love and they're ready to lead us home to peace.

I've been fascinated by religion ever since I was young, but I've learned that even though we have it down here on Earth, it's not actually something that exists in heaven. Angels have taught me through my daily practice that all belief systems are just different roads to the same place: love. All that remains in heaven is love – it's a space of utter peace and acceptance and these divine beings can help us create it on Earth. We start within.

We can call on any of these figures without having to believe in the religion to which they may or may not be connected – they are more than that. Ultimately, they are the divine's representation of complete and utter acceptance.

We've already met a handful of the angels and ascended masters who are able to help us with forgiveness. In order for you to continue with your practice, I thought it would be helpful to have a space in this book where you could come and commune with these masters directly.

Even though I've called these beings 'masters', that doesn't mean they are more special than we are and it doesn't mean we should worship them. It is more that they're figures we can respect and call on, because they've either walked the path that we're walking now or they've dedicated themselves to serving humanity.

Every person we meet will have a different face – their shell will be different – but when we look within, we are all light, all the essence of love. Ascended masters are beings who have recognized that light and are here to help us recognize it within ourselves and others, too. They are here to help us forgive.

In this chapter, I've drawn together the angels and masters I feel will be of assistance in this process. These are beings I'm particularly drawn to and have called on during my spiritual practice – it would be wrong of me to list those I haven't actually had a connection with – but the list doesn't end here. You can call out to any saints, loved ones, goddesses and gods who resonate with you.

For those of you who find it difficult to relate to a specific being rather than the energy of oneness, look at it like this: these beings represent oneness and they represent universal love. In my eyes, they are universal consciousness expressed in a way that we can understand and have a personal relationship with.

If you find it difficult to believe in a particular master or saint, remember that people from all over the world call on these beings with great faith and reverence in their hearts. Even if they aren't 'real', this belief alone makes the energy connected to them so powerful that it would be a great loss for it to go to waste, so welcome it into your life.

Ascended Masters

Jesus

Jesus is the bringer of truth. He is a light to the entire universe and a living/dying/spiritual demonstration that forgiveness is possible. When he lived and walked the Earth, he was persecuted for his beliefs and teachings, yet he still loved his brothers and sisters of this Earth.

Jesus is everywhere at once. He is with you right now. He waits for your call and with the help of his holy angels, he can restore you to your natural light-filled self.

When you call on Jesus, he will bring light to your mind and help you to see. His presence removes all the blindfolds that prevent you from seeing and all the blockages that stand between you and the miracle you seek. He is the voice of love and his presence echoes in your heart, waiting for you to accept that you are forgiven. He helps you to see the light in others, so you can live a life that's filled with miracles and free from condemnation.

Jesus may be a spiritual teacher, but he loves to be recognized as a friend and a brother. He comes to you as an equal and he doesn't ask you to idolize him but to see that what he has, you have, too. Jesus is the voice of spirit that helps you to see that forgiveness is the *only* choice of your soul – he helps you to eradicate the voice of fear.

Your light is never lost – it is always present – but with life's challenges it is very easily forgotten and hidden. When you think of Jesus, he comes like a blazing torch into your holy temple, lighting it up so you can see clearly. With his presence alone, he will light up all the darkness so you can move into the acceptance and forgiveness of God.

Call on Jesus to help you with:

- healing
- forgiving those who have hurt you, either emotionally or physically
- remembering that love is real
- accepting that God's only plan for you is love

Here is a prayer to Jesus:

'*Dear Jesus,*

Thank you for standing in the forefront of my mind and helping me see the truth. Like a blazing torch, your light extends to the four corners of my being, removing all darkness and doubt.

Into your presence I enter now and I welcome your unconditional acceptance and love as I realize that forgiveness is a natural part of who I am, because it is remembering that as a being of light I can never really be hurt. I am safe, Jesus, and I know that you are my loving guide.

I welcome you now to point out any areas of myself and my life that require my forgiveness. With your support, I make the miraculous choice to forgive and be forgiven.

Thank you, my friend and brother.

And so it is!'

Mary Magdalene

To me, Mary Magdalene is the female who balances Jesus's masculine energy. She is an amazing woman who once walked the Earth and, just like her friend/teacher/peer Jesus, she found her beliefs, teachings and clairvoyant vision scrutinized and questioned by others. She knows what it's like to forgive.

Mary Magdalene is the ascended one who can relate to our humanity, because she also was challenged by her emotional self. She, too, wept when she experienced loss and when others cast doubt on her teaching. But with strength, courage, determination and faith, she reclaimed her power to teach and heal.

Mary comes to you and helps you to stand tall and be a leader of love. The essence of the Magdalene enters the cave of your heart and helps to awaken your ability to stand up for what you believe in. She helps you follow your soul's truth even if it's under scrutiny. She is the perfect leader for all lightworkers.

The energy of Magdalene and her angels also helps to awaken your inner vision. She helps you to tear down all the barriers that the ego has convinced you to hide behind. She helps you realize that in order to reach peace you have to release all ideas of conflict and attack. They are not natural to you. Mary helps you stand in your true essence – love – and share it with the world.

Invoking the presence of Mary Magdalene will bring about great shifts in your life. She won't only help you understand what forgiveness is, she will help you *live* the path of forgiveness. Mary's message comes to you at this time and she reminds you that the soul is indestructible and that you have the ability to stand strong with integrity. She is fiercely forgiving and she will help you be, too.

Call on Mary Magdalene to help you with:

- honouring your gifts
- understanding forgiveness
- overcoming doubt
- reconnecting to the guidance of your heart
- opening up your clairvoyant abilities

Here is a prayer to Mary Magdalene:

'Mary of Magdala, you who are known as the Magdalene,

Thank you for drawing close to me at this time. I welcome your essence into the cave of my heart as you ignite within me the ability to forgive and be forgiven.

I am ready now to follow in your footsteps and stand within my power to serve humanity and be a leader of love.

I thank you for silencing the voice of the ego with your fierce ruby light and for amplifying the voice of spirit so I can follow my spiritual truth. I welcome your protection and strength.

Thank you for being my sister in the light. Your help is welcome here now!

And so it is!'

Mary the Divine Mother

Mary the mother of Jesus has always been a real figure of love in my life. My first encounter with her, as I related earlier, was at church with my neighbour, who was saying a prayer and lighting a candle for my dying grandmother. I've always believed that even though Mary has strong links to the Catholic faith, she is a figure of unconditional love whom anyone can call on, no matter what their creed, religion or gender. She comes to all who reach out to her with complete and utter acceptance in her heart.

This powerful figure is also known as the Queen of the Angels, because she works tirelessly with the angelic realm to bring about peace, forgiveness and unconditional love. She is a force that we can all relate to because we've all had a mother, grandmother or other maternal figure of some sort in our life.

Mary looks upon every man, woman, boy and girl as her own. She sees each of us as her child. With her bright blue light of purification and protection, she makes us feel safe. Like a huge, loving hug, she comes right into our soul and reminds us that love is our natural state. She washes away any feelings of resentment and resistance that hold us back from a happier and more balanced life.

Call on Mary the Divine Mother to help you with:

- removing fears that stand between you and forgiveness
- all aspects of forgiveness in parenting and motherhood
- feeling safe and protected
- receiving a boost of confidence and love
- manifesting forgiveness in places in need

Here is a prayer to the Divine Mother:

'Divine Mother Mary, Queen of the Angels and mother of our planet,

Thank you for bestowing your blessings of peace on and through my life. With your support, I know that forgiveness is the way forward for me and this planet.

Thank you for drawing close and wrapping your blue cloak of wisdom around me as I release all harsh judgements about myself, others and this planet. I feel safe and nurtured by your love as I choose forgiveness and set myself free.

And so it is!'

Buddha

The word 'Buddha' means 'awakened one' and that's certainly what happened to Siddharta Gautama, as he was once known. He was a wealthy Indian prince whose father mollycoddled him and protected him from the real world and the suffering that took place within it, but one day the prince asked his horseman to take him outside the castle grounds and encountered an old man, a sick man and a dead man – and he just couldn't understand what was happening.

Later that night, the prince left his home and his wealth behind and went out to search for something that would put a stop to the suffering of the world and bring peace to humanity.

During his search, he went from one extreme to the other. Having started out with his every need fulfilled, he stripped himself of all his belongings and lived an ascetic lifestyle, at one point existing on just three sesame seeds per day. But he still didn't find what he was looking for. It was then that he decided to sit underneath a bodhi tree until he found complete enlightenment.

Under the bodhi tree, the Buddha was faced with the fears and desires of his ego, but he kept his attention on his breath and peace in his heart. And it was then that he reached enlightenment through non-attachment.

The Buddha can help you to detach from the voice of fear and the desire for things that aren't serving you. He can help you to accept what has happened and what you cannot change. Then you can begin transforming where you are today.

Call on the Buddha to help you:

- stop going down the same old road
- eliminate your desire for situations that aren't serving you
- detach from the fears your ego mind feeds you
- find the peace that rests within you

Here's a prayer to the Buddha:

'Buddha, Enlightened One and friend,

Thank you for your guidance and support as I welcome your peace and tranquillity into my heart at this time.

Thank you for helping me to let go of my past and the desires that no longer serve my purpose, which is to find peace.

I welcome you to light my way so I can detach from the fears of my ego mind, arrive in the paradise of my soul and share that paradise with everyone I meet.

I welcome you, dear Buddha, into my heart so I can be loving and accepting, just like you.

And so it is!'

Tara

Tara is a Buddhist goddess who brings compassion and protection from all harm. She is known as the Mother of Liberation and her name means 'diamond'.

In Tibetan Buddhism, Tara is a bodhisattva, which is basically an angelic being who comes to those in need and supports them through their challenges here on Earth. A boddhisattva is said to have reached a state of enlightenment through compassion for others.

The tale that tells of the birth of Tara is a beautiful and esoteric one. It is said she was born from the tears of Avalokiteshvara, the lord of compassion, when he was looking down on the world and seeing people suffering. His tears fell like thunderbolts and from one of them grew a lotus that opened up with Tara inside. Her whole essence is said to support us, guiding us from suffering and shame to compassion and liberation.

I see Tara as an angelic golden being. She comes to all of us on Earth who find it difficult to understand others and their circumstances. In terms of forgiveness, she guides us to freedom by enabling us to see another person's point of view. She helps us to see that people only hurt others when they are in fear.

With Tara's support, you can have compassion for those who have hurt you and can hope they find peace through your forgiveness. In this way you can release the pain caused by their poor choices.

Tara has many forms and they're all associated with colours. White Tara is associated with purification, Green Tara protects us from all types of harm and Golden Tara fulfils wishes and brings prosperity.

Call on Tara to help you:

- feel safe when you're being judged or misunderstood
- have compassion for others
- liberate yourself from resentment

- serve humanity through loving acts
- activate your inner Buddha

Here's a prayer to Tara:

'Tara, Mother of all Buddhas,

Thank you for drawing close at this time and for illuminating the areas in my life where I can be more compassionate and like you.

I am ready to leave behind all harsh judgements of others and myself – I am ready to serve humanity through the peace I create within.

With your angelic golden, white and green rays, you offer your support and I welcome it, and your guidance, too.

Oh, goddess of compassion, thank you for moving your kindness through me.

And so it is!'

Krishna

Krishna is one of India's best-loved deities. He is said to be the incarnation of the god Vishnu, who is part of the Indian trinity, and he is completely devoted to peace for all sentient beings throughout time and space.

Krishna is best known for his role in the spiritual text the *Bhagavad Gita*, where he acts as a guide and mentor to Arjuna, a man who is about to enter a great war with his cousins. Krishna helps Arjuna to make his own moral and ethical decisions without telling him the right choice to make – and for that reason he has been called on by many who are seeking clarity.

Whenever I think of Krishna, I feel utter love, kindness and peace in my heart. He is a sensitive master who wants everyone to follow the pathway of love.

Tales of his life depict him as a wonderful consort to the goddess Radha, whom he absolutely adores, so he can also be called on for help with relationships and forgiveness in the area of love.

Krishna is often portrayed in gardens with wild animals, so he can help you with forgiveness in the context of animals. For example, if you've seen an animal be hurt and you're finding it hard to forgive the perpetrator or you're working with an animal to overcome fear from its past, Krishna will help and support you.

I had an encounter with Krishna while in India. I was staying on an organic farm in southern India when one of the staff began to hit a dog I'd fallen in love with. I ran to the dog's rescue and swept the man off his feet. Out of complete anger, frustration and fear, I stood on his chest and gave him a massive fright. The dog thankfully was OK and I looked after her for the rest of the trip.

After the incident, I got very frustrated and ran to the temple. I found myself falling on my knees in front of the Radha and Krishna statues and sobbing.

All of a sudden, peace came over me. I closed my eyes and felt my body being bathed in a light of peace. In that moment I knew that forgiveness was the only option. Krishna helped me to see that I couldn't hang on to what had happened and I couldn't force fear onto someone else. I needed to demonstrate what it meant to forgive.

The next morning I approached the man and he opened his arms to hug me. It seemed that whatever had happened between me, him and Lord Krishna had affected his heart, too.

I remember telling him that I was sorry and even though he couldn't speak a word of English, I knew he understood. He placed his hands in prayer position and bowed to me. Best of all, it seems he knew that he needed to be more respectful to the dog and from then on he was good to her. Thank you, Krishna!

You can call on Krishna to help you:

- make the right decisions in a particular situation
- forgive relationships past and present
- move past the resentment that stops you from accepting love
- heal anything to do with romantic/soul-mate relationships
- work through forgiveness with animals and pets

Here's a prayer to Krishna:

'Krishna, lord of light and teacher of kindness,

Thank you for drawing close to me at this time. I welcome your loving support and guidance as I begin to work through forgiveness in all areas of my life. Thank you for bringing to my attention areas of my life that need decisions and for leading me to the decisions that serve my purpose and humanity.

Thank you for teaching me that loving relationships can be conscious, too.

I am blessed to have your support.

And so it is!'

Shiva

Shiva's name means 'the auspicious one' and he is seen as one of the primary forms of God in Hinduism. He is a powerful image of the divine and is one of the three main faces of the Hindu trinity (the other two being Brahma and Vishnu).

Shiva is known as the destroyer god, but in more recent times has been named 'the transformer' because he can be called upon to transform a negative situation.

Shiva has many forms, each with their own personality type and name. He has been known as Mahadeva, which means 'Great God', and also Nataraja, 'the cosmic dancer'.

Shiva's main purpose is to destroy a weary universe and prepare the way for Brahma to begin the process of creation. In the context of forgiveness, he is a wonderful master to call on to prepare the way for you. He can help you to create a new beginning in your life.

Shiva has been seen as a wrathful deity because of his fiery, destructive nature, but the truth is he is a being of unconditional love. In my *Angel Prayers Oracle* deck I have dedicated 'The Divine Father' card to Shiva. The artist helped me to create a peaceful, loving figure who was powerful at the same time. In this image Shiva has four arms: two are holding the sun with the 'Om' symbol, representing oneness and life, and the other two are in a position of prayer to show Shiva honouring us. He has a snake around his neck, showing he has tamed the viciousness of his ego, and a drum to wake up his wandering mind.

When I was in India I stayed in a town called Tiruvannamalai, which is host to a holy site dedicated to Shiva. There is a temple called Annamalaiyar, which is at the foot of a holy hill called Arunachala, where Shiva is said to manifest. I went to the hill and walked up it with a group of other pilgrims. We started at

7 a.m. and it took me two hours, but it can take people up to four. Almost at the top of the hill there is a group of devotees to Shiva who encourage you to take your shoes off to go to the very top. It is there that you can walk in the footsteps of Shiva. I felt held, supported and energized from the climb and I knew Shiva's presence was strong there.

You can call on Shiva to help you:

- clear the pathway to forgiveness
- remove the fears and wickedness of your ego
- regain your sense of oneness with all living beings
- restore your faith in God
- remove any resentment towards God
- heal any issues with fatherhood

There is a mantra to Shiva that I've found to be very powerful. I learned it at the Mind, Body, Spirit Festival on 11.11.11 and it has been popping up all over the world ever since. In fact, many of the men climbing the Arunachala hill in India were chanting it out loud. Traditional Indian chants are done 108 times. The mantra is *Om Nama Shivaya* (pronounced 'Ommm Namah Sheeevayah').

Here is a prayer to Shiva:

'Lord Shiva, cosmic dancer and transformer,

Thank you for drawing close and for preparing the path to forgiveness for me.

I welcome you now to bring to my attention ways of removing the wickedness and vicious comments of my ego so I can restore my natural connection to the oneness of all sentient beings.

Thank you for coming close like a peaceful father figure and helping me to feel safe as I move along the path to my divine purpose, which is to be happy.

And so it is!'

Kali

Kali is a Hindu goddess who brings a real sense of empowerment and strength. She is seen as one of the wrathful incarnations of Shiva's wife, Parvati, and even though she's not a goddess to be messed with, she's a great ally to all those who call on her. Her name means 'Black' or 'End of Time' and she is regarded as the goddess of death.

When you see images of Kali you'll see her as a blue or black-skinned goddess with eight arms. She will be holding weapons in those arms and may even have a necklace of skulls. She will most likely be standing on top of a man, Shiva, who is said to tame her destructive anger with his presence.

Because of her image, Kali is feared by many spiritual practitioners. The idea of calling on a wrathful goddess associated with death can be a lot to handle and Kali does bring a sense of the unknown, just like death itself.

In my eyes, however, Kali is a goddess figure to call on for help in coming to terms with the idea that not everything you see on Earth is permanent. She helps you to remove attachments to physical things so you can enhance your connection to the deeper spiritual aspects of your being.

I believe Kali is the same force as the Black Madonna. She will consume all of your fear. She will look into the eyes of your soul and ask you if you are ready to move away from the challenging and destructive thoughts and situations that are blocking your pathway to truth and forgiveness.

Kali really is a benevolent mother figure, but like most mothers she has the fire in her belly to give you a shake if you need one. In the context of forgiveness, she's a wonderful figure to call on to remove the parts of you that are self-destructive, for example the parts that keep going back to a relationship that's breaking your heart or feeding an addiction that's not serving you.

Kali will scare away your fear. She will strip from your soul any aspects that aren't serving your growth and she will tame your ego so much that she'll put her foot right on top of it. She'll come to you like a loving mother and tell you you're forgiven, but she'll also tell you to leave the past where it is and move on.

Call on Kali to help you with:

- removing self-destructive patterns from your life
- taming angry thoughts
- taking a stand in negative situations
- removing all aspects of fear
- enhancing your powerful feminine side

Here's a prayer to Kali:

'Kali, mother goddess,

I call on you now and welcome your help in eliminating the darkness from my life. Thank you for removing the destructive patterns in my personality and for taming the angry thoughts that stand between me and the state of forgiveness.

Come into me now and empower me to move forward in a fearless way.

It feels so good to know your loving, protective essence is with me now.

And so it is!'

Ganesh

Ganesh is the Indian elephant god who is revered all over the world. He's known as the remover of obstacles because of his unique ability to remove obstacles from our path to inner peace.

Ganesh is the son of Shiva and Parvati. Legend tells us that he got his elephant head after a horrific accident that happened at his home. Shiva was out one day with his powerful army and Parvati was at home doing bits and bobs around the house. She got bored, so she decided to mould a little boy out of clay. Once she had done this, she loved the model so much she used her powers to bring him to life and called him Ganesh.

Realizing that the clay had got everywhere, Parvati left Ganesh to guard the home while she went to get washed. While she was doing that, Shiva came home and found what he thought to be an imposter in his home. With one sweep of his sword, he took off Ganesh's head.

Parvati was so upset when she found out what had happened. Shiva couldn't console her, so he sent out his guards and told them to bring him the head of the first living being they found that was facing east. The guards found an elephant and brought its head back, and Shiva used it to bring Ganesh back to life with a new face.

Even though this story is more like a fairytale than a historical event, it shows that Ganesh's energy has the ability to bring us back to life, even if we feel we've lost our head in a situation.

I've been drawn to Ganesh for years. I've always kept him close in my spiritual practice because whenever I've been faced with an obstacle, I've called on him. He seems to come right in and sweep away any challenges that stand before me.

I travel with a Ganesh picture whenever I'm out of the country and I kept a postcard of him by my yoga mat all the way through yoga training. He's always been a great figure of peace for me. Not only that, my favourite wild animal is the elephant. I love the fact that elephants are family and community-orientated beings and in Ganesh's honour I donate to Save the Elephants every month.

Ganesh can help to remove obstacles in all areas of your life. In the context of forgiveness, he'll help you to get around any thoughts that are preventing you from forgiving either yourself or another person. He can help you to get around any blocks with making peace with others, too.

You can call on Ganesh for assistance with:

- removing blocks and obstacles in your life
- smoothing your path
- awakening your sense of connectedness with your community
- removing the busyness of challenging thoughts

Here's a prayer to Ganesh:

'Ganesh,

Thank you for standing before me and removing all the obstacles on my path. It feels so comforting to know that your gentle and humane soul is lovingly clearing the path before me.

With your support, I now step onto the pathway of forgiveness, acceptance and peace. From this strong and healthy place I create a life that is filled with blessings and abundance.

Thank you for lighting the way. I am following you now.

And so it is!'

The Angels of Forgiveness

The angels of forgiveness are a force of angels you can call on at any time. They will come to you and prompt you through an inner voice or instinct. They will lovingly help you, with grace, to release any painful illusions. They will guide you to see that you are a brilliant light and what happens here on Earth isn't the full truth. Through forgiveness, these amazing angels will help you to remember that you are a holy and wholly loved child of God.

You have a guardian angel of forgiveness who is standing by you now. Whether you've realized it or not, there are areas of your life where forgiveness is needed. The angel of forgiveness standing by you has prompted you to think of these areas and is waiting to see whether you will choose to listen.

Your angel of forgiveness waits in the centre of your heart. They don't need a name and they don't need a fancy prayer, they just need you to be present. They need you to be *in* the present. The present is where you can assess not how far you've come and not where you're going, but the beauty of where you are today. It's not about planning ahead or remembering what's happened, but about enjoying the beautiful view of the here and now.

Your forgiveness angel invites you to be still, to enjoy the silence and to breathe. It is in these moments that they can help you to become gracefully aware of your inner divinity, your wholeness and the peace that awaits you.

The angels of forgiveness don't understand conflict, because it isn't real. They ask you to let go of all the thoughts that stand between you and happiness. These thoughts and feelings are driven by your ego, which wants to be right and wishes to prove a point. It wants those who have hurt you to suffer. It's driven by fear. Your angel, on the other hand, summons you into your heart and helps you see that there is no enemy there – only love.

Your angel presents you with a holy vision of reality: the real you, the healed you, the held and supported you. It wants you to see what they see – and they see you as whole, healed and complete.

Sit in silence, remove all distractions, turn off all phones, step away from the 'real' world and spend some time in your heart.

Close your eyes and say this prayer:

'Into the cave of my heart would I enter now to meet the shining face of my guardian angel of forgiveness.

And so it is!'

The Angels of Peace

There is a congregation of angels who are dedicated to the peace of this planet. They work directly with the Divine Mother Mary. These beings are some of the gentlest and most beautiful angels I've ever seen. They are made of golden, white and pearlescent light. They move in and out of the air like a drop of paint falling into water. Wherever they go, they bring the scent of roses, sweet lilies and lavender.

These angels are dedicated to the peace of every sentient being on this planet. They respond to the call of grace that every soul can make. The call of grace is like an SOS, because it's when the soul sends a call for help to heaven. And it's these angels who often save people, animals and countries through dramatic and miraculous intervention.

Peace angels can bring the forgiveness mindset to entire nations. They can send their light to world leaders and those in power – they're just waiting to be asked.

A beautiful thing I've found about these angels is the fact that they can respond to any prayer, even if it's not addressed directly to them. They hear any plea for peace by any sentient being on the planet and respond to a call from any heart that desires serenity for all living beings.

I believe the peace angels are present when the most blessed things happen, for example when you see a dog save a kitten from drowning or a wolf form a friendship with a donkey. They inspire us to love each other and see brother or sister in our neighbour.

I've seen angels of peace weep with joy, especially when their mission is complete. Just this year I met a lady who told me how she was saved by an angel from a horrific car crash. As she told me the story, I began to cry. Tears of joy rolled down my face because behind her I could see an angel weeping in celebration because her life had been spared and she could continue to inspire others.

Call on the angels of peace and let their blessings unfold throughout humanity with the following prayer:

'Dear angels of peace,

Thank you for extending your waves of kindness, acceptance and love to all hearts that are open to peace.

Thank you for guiding healing and peaceful light to the children and animals of this planet, who sometimes don't have a voice. Thank you for shining upon their path.

I allow you to show me how I can bring healing, change and forgiveness to this planet and all its inhabitants.

And so it is!'

The Myriam

Hopefully by this point you've thought about, reached out to or even encountered the Myriam. You'll remember that these angels were the guardian angels of Mary Magdalene and have chosen to continue working with her from heaven to bring about radical shifts on Earth and healing to humanity.

The Myriam make me feel so overwhelmed with love. They have a real essence of purity about them. They're the most beautiful beings I've ever seen. They're like twin flames, dancing and weaving through the air in their pearlescent robes.

I'll never forget seeing them work with a group. Just this year I did a presentation about Mary Magdalene and her Gnostic Gospel to a gathering of 40 people. I told them about my encounters with the Myriam and how I felt they were dedicated to removing grief and all the challenging emotions surrounding it.

I led the group on a deep, emotional and light-filled meditation where they could open themselves up to the Myriam's help. I had my eyes closed, but could hear cries and deep sobs of relief as these graceful angels entered the hearts of all of those present. When I opened my eyes to check everyone was OK, I could see people wiping tears from their eyes while pure white lights were swirling all around them. I knew that healing was taking place.

After the meditation we had a group discussion and many people said they'd realized while invoking the Myriam where they had grievances stored away. One woman admitted she always gave herself a hard time over her naked body – she'd look at herself in the mirror and sadness and frustration would wash over her. Another woman spoke of the pain of losing a close family member and confessed that to this day she felt responsible, though matters had really been out of her hands. The Myriam helped these people to release their grief – that's why the tears were present.

The Myriam will help you, too. They come with a divine white light and will wash the three aspects of your being with it: your physical body will be covered in their light, the altar of your mind will be cleared by the light and the wholeness of your soul will be seen in the light.

These angels will also awaken within you the vision of Christ – they will help you to see everyone as an equal, everyone as a soul. They will help you to remember that you're not separate from your loved ones and that all those who have gone to heaven before you are actually waiting in the centre of your heart. The Myriam bring miraculous healing on a spiritual scale and they wait for your call.

You can invoke them in many ways. One of these is drawing the *vesica piscis (see page 58)*. Or you may like to say the following prayer:

'The Beloved Myriam,

I welcome you now to stand in the forefront of my mind and show me the areas of my life that require a miracle. Thank you for helping me to see where the grievances are present in my life so I can release them.

I am ready to see the light of Christ in all. I am ready to forgive and accept all of humanity. The time is now. May my vision of holiness awaken now!

I am blessed to have you on my left and right while guiding me from within.

And so it is!'

Chapter 12
ACCEPTING THE MIRACLE

'Your task is not to seek for love, but merely to seek and find all the barriers within yourself that you have built against it.'
A COURSE IN MIRACLES

So, where now? It's inevitable that life is going to throw you a curveball when it comes to forgiveness. But there's a great chance that you've come to this book because you know that forgiveness is going to lead you to peace, and that is the first step. I really believe that it's all about intention – that's probably more important than the process. When we intend to do something we will eventually get there, and it doesn't matter how long it takes us.

During the writing of this book I've uncovered many areas of my life that have required forgiveness and I've become more aware of how to move into forgiveness. I really believe that writing about forgiveness has brought me to a deeper awareness of this amazing process and how we go through it.

Touching Hearts

While I was writing this book, I was blessed to be able to spend some final moments with one of my clients who became a friend. She was a young woman called Michelle, a member of my Angel Club who was always a brilliant light. I knew from her friends that Michelle was having a hard time with cancer. Initially she'd overcome the dis-ease, but it had come back and this time unfortunately it was proving too much for her body to handle.

Just weeks before she went to heaven, I hosted a Mother Mary day in my office for a few friends and we held intentions and healing thoughts for the world. Michelle plucked up the energy and courage to join us and little did I know it would be the last time we got to hang out. Even though she was near the end of her life, she had so much faith in angels and in life itself that she helped to bring a smile to everyone who met her.

I remember going to her funeral service in East Kilbride, near Glasgow, and sharing tears at such a loss to this world. She was barely 40 and it made me wonder why things like this happen, but also gave me a massive reminder that even though Michelle had gone early, she'd done what she needed to do: love.

Everywhere she went, Michelle was a force of love. Even though I only knew her for just over a year, I knew she'd inspired many people. When she left, though she may have broken the hearts of those who were closest to her, she helped them, and me, to remember that it's not worth living a life with sadness and resentment. She certainly helped me to remember that love is the only way.

There's a chance that you've lost someone in your life, perhaps someone very close to you. Let them be your loving reminder that life is worth living and life is worth *forgiving* – because it helps you be the love you are.

Guidance from a Friend

After Michelle's funeral, I went for lunch with my friend Georgina, who'd come to the funeral with me. Georgina is another Angel Club member who'd joined me in my office to invoke Mother Mary that day. We have so much in common – she, too, practises Ashtanga yoga and follows *A Course in Miracles*.

During lunch we spoke about many different subjects, including forgiveness and how important it is to accept it in our lives. Georgina also told me about a family member of hers who was being bothered by their ex-partner, who was causing hassle just because he could. Before I knew it, I was shaking my head and moving into a space of judgement.

'He sounds like a…' I started.

But before I could finish my sentence, Georgina said, 'Joy!' with a huge smile on her face.

What a powerful and affirmative way to be! I asked Georgina if I could share her guidance with you and she agreed, so here it is:

'The next time you feel yourself about to call someone a name or have an unforgiving opinion about them in your mind, just call them "a joy" instead of, well, something worse. When you move into the state of forgiveness, you remember everyone's purity and innocence and you remember that they are a creation of love (even if they've forgotten, it's your job to remember).'

What more can I say?!

Reassessing the Miracle

By this point I hope you've realized that forgiveness isn't just something you say and isn't just something you do.

It's a state you enter:

> Forgiveness is a state where you remember your innocence.

> Forgiveness is a state where you recognize you are indestructible.

> Forgiveness is a state where you remember you are pure light.

It's a remembering process:

> Forgiveness is remembering that sin is not real.

> Forgiveness is remembering that only love is real.

> Forgiveness is remembering you are not separate from the divine.

It's an aspect of the divine:

> When you forgive, angels draw close.

> When you forgive, you lift your heart to God.

> When you forgive, you return to your natural state of wholeness.

Here's a final message, sent to you from love:

'You may not recognize me and you may not know who I am. Let me help you to remember.

I've been with you since the beginning. Before you entered time and space, I knew who you were. I've watched you since the seed was planted deep in your mother's womb. I watched you grow from the single strand of DNA. I was with you as you developed and prepared to enter the world. I was there at your birth. I have travelled with you since your first steps and I will be with you when you take your last breath.

When I look at you, I see beyond your skin. I don't just see your organs and I don't recognize your flaws. When I look at you, I see a being bursting with light. I see you filled with unlimited potential. I look at you and wonder why you get so upset, stressed, frustrated and mad. I look at you and hope that one day you will see what I see. I see a body, but within that I see a soul. I see you as a child, but I know you as a friend.

I am here to serve you gladly and I wait for you to call. I have seen you through your challenges, I have seen you rise and fall. I have never forgotten you and I hope you will remember me, because I'm standing right here with you now.

We were together once and we danced among the stars. I am here now to tell you something that I really want you to know.

You are free and innocent. You are as perfect as can be. You have not let down life, the Creator or me. You are forgiven already – you don't need to ask. All you have to do is accept it, but that's no easy task. Are you ready to accept it? Because I'm telling you the truth and I am your guardian angel.

You are forgiven. It is time to accept it. You are love. Love holds no boundaries. You are unbound, whole, complete and healed. Love is who you are. I love you.'

ACKNOWLEDGEMENTS

I had a great deal of support around me while writing this book – it was probably the most enlightening and challenging project of my life.

I was sitting in a barber's chair on the phone to Michelle Pilley when I pitched my idea for the book, and she instantly gave me the go ahead. I am so grateful to have a Publisher like you, Michelle – you are a channel of love.

I'd also like to extend my thanks to Robert Holden, who as far as I'm concerned is the best mentor, coach, friend and wine expert I could ever know. Robert helped me reach a new level of understanding with *A Course in Miracles* and with myself – he even helped me find the title of this book. Thank you also for introducing me to your family; they have become people I adore. I love you, Bobby!

Gabrielle – what can I say? I am so blessed to know you. Thank you for writing such a beautiful foreword. You touch my heart and soul every time I see you and I'm grateful to be on this journey with you. You are an earth angel.

I'd like to thank Lizzie, my editor – you're a wizard. Thanks for taking my work and making it 10 times better than before.

I'd also like to thank Julie Oughton at Hay House for her patience and guidance, and Leanne for working miracles on the cover and internal design.

Big shouts and loving hugs to Ruth and Jo at Hay House for keeping me in the press, and for truly believing in this work. You guys put yourself out there all the time for me and I'm grateful to have amazing support from you.

Thanks to Sara Twigger for coming to Glastonbury with me and helping me to understand the miracles that forgiveness offers. To Meggan Watterson – thank you for initiating me to the Goddess. Kate & Mike Watts – staying with you in Maine was sincerely the best time EVER. You two are my role models in life and in love.

Jason – thanks for the epic cover art. It's splendid.

Dad – thanks for your support. I also love how you're getting into this stuff more and more.

Finally, Mum – you are my rock, my biggest fan and my greatest support. I am so glad the angels helped me pick you to guide me along this path. You are the best psychic I know and the person who tries to learn this stuff better than me so you can help me grow. I love you so much.

ABOUT THE AUTHOR

Drew John Barnes

Kyle Gray has had spiritual encounters from an early age. When he was just four years old, his grandmother's soul visited him from beyond the grave.

Growing up, Kyle always had an ability to hear, feel and see what goes beyond the natural senses, which eventually led him to discovering the power and love of angels in his teens.

Now, at just 26, Kyle is one of the most hip and sought-after experts in his field. With his unique ability to stay grounded and keep it real, he re-introduces the idea of angels in a modern and accessible way. Kyle's talks in the UK and around Europe sell out within days, and his private sessions have a two-year waiting list. He is the author of four books.

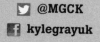

🐦 **@MGCK**

📘 **kylegrayuk**

www.kylegray.co.uk